Hilary Patrinos
1978.

D1355693

REGENTS RESTORATION DRAMA SERIES

General Editor: John Loftis

THE PROVOKED WIFE

SIR JOHN VANBRUGH

The Provoked Wife

Edited by

CURT A. ZIMANSKY

EDWARD ARNOLD

Cloth edition: ISBN 0 7131 5569 8
Paper edition: ISBN 0 7131 5570 1

Printed in Great Britain by
William Clowes and Sons, Limited, London and Beccles

Regents Restoration Drama Series

The Regents Restoration Drama Series provides soundly edited texts, in modern spelling, of the more significant plays of the late seventeenth and early eighteenth centuries. The word "Restoration" is here used ambiguously and must be explained. If to the historian it refers to the period between 1660 and 1685 (or 1688), it has long been used by the student of drama in default of a more precise word to refer to plays belonging to the dramatic tradition established in the 1660's, weakening after 1700, and displaced in the 1730's. It is in this extended sense—imprecise though justified by academic custom—that the word is used in this series, which includes plays first produced between 1660 and 1737. Although these limiting dates are determined by political events, the return of Charles II (and the removal of prohibitions against operation of theaters) and the passage of Walpole's Stage Licensing Act, they enclose a period of dramatic history having a coherence of its own in the establishment, development, and disintegration of a tradition.

Some twenty editions having appeared as this volume goes to press, the series has reached nearly a half of its anticipated range of between forty and fifty volumes. The volumes will continue to be published for a number of years, at the rate of three or more annually. From the beginning the editors have planned the series with attention to the projected dimensions of the completed whole, a representative collection of Restoration drama providing a record of artistic achievement and providing also a record of the deepest concerns of three generations of Englishmen. And thus it contains deservedly famous plays—*The Country Wife*, *The Man of Mode*, and *The Way of the World*—and also significant but little known plays, *The Virtuoso*, for example, and *City Politiques*, the former a satirical review of scientific investigation in the early years of the Royal Society, the latter an equally satirical review of politics at the time of the Popish Plot. If the volumes of famous plays finally achieve the larger circulation, the other volumes may conceivably have the greater utility, in making available texts otherwise difficult of access with the editorial apparatus needed to make them intelligible.

The editors have had the instructive example of the parallel and senior project, the Regents Renaissance Drama Series; they have in fact used the editorial policies developed for the earlier plays as their own, modifying them as appropriate for the later period and as the experience of successive editions suggested. The introductions to the separate Restoration plays differ considerably in their nature. Although a uniform body of relevant information is presented in each of them, no attempt has been made to impose a pattern of interpretation. Emphasis in the introductions has necessarily varied with the nature of the plays and inevitably—we think desirably—with the special interests and aptitudes of the different editors.

Each text in the series is based on a fresh collation of the seventeenth- and eighteenth-century editions that might be presumed to have authority. The textual notes, which appear above the rule at the bottom of each page, record all substantive departures from the edition used as the copy-text. Variant substantive readings among contemporary editions are listed there as well. Editions later than the eighteenth century are referred to in the textual notes only when an emendation originating in some one of them is received into the text. Variants of accidentals (spelling, punctuation, capitalization) are not recorded in the notes. Contracted forms of characters' names are silently expanded in speech prefixes and stage directions and, in the case of speech prefixes, are regularized. Additions to the stage directions of the copy-text are enclosed in brackets.

Spelling has been modernized along consciously conservative lines, but within the limits of a modernized text the linguistic quality of the original has been carefully preserved. Contracted preterites have regularly been expanded. Punctuation has been brought into accord with modern practices. The objective has been to achieve a balance between the pointing of the old editions and a system of punctuation which, without overloading the text with exclamation marks, semicolons, and dashes, will make the often loosely flowing verse and prose of the original syntactically intelligible to the modern reader. Dashes are regularly used only to indicate interrupted speeches, or shifts of address within a single speech.

Explanatory notes, chiefly concerned with glossing obsolete words and phrases, are printed below the textual notes at the bottom of each page. References to stage directions in the notes follow the admirable system of the Revels editions, whereby stage directions are keyed, decimally, to the line of the text before or after which they occur. Thus, a note on 0.2 has reference to the second line of the stage direction at the beginning of the scene in question. A note on 115.1 has reference to the first line of the stage direction following line 115 of the text of the relevant scene. Speech prefixes, and any stage directions attached to them, are keyed to the first line of accompanying dialogue.

JOHN LOFTIS

March, 1969
Stanford University

Contents

List of Abbreviations

P   *Plays Written by Sir John Vanbrugh*. 2 vols. London, 1719.

Q1   First Quarto, 1697.

Q2   Second Quarto, 1698.

Q3   Third Quarto, 1709.

Introduction

The first edition of *The Provoked Wife* (Q1) was advertised in the *Post Boy*, May 11–13, 1697; presumably the book was published within a month of the first performance. As with his other plays, Vanbrugh appears not to have overseen either this or subsequent editions. Still, the text is excellent, and a few press corrections show that some care was taken.[1] There was a second edition in 1698 (Q2), and this was reprinted line for line in 1709 (Q3). The printing in the first volume of Vanbrugh's *Plays* in 1719 completes the list of editions that could even remotely be thought to have authority.[2] All are good, and the text deteriorates very little from printing to printing. The present edition departs from Q1 only where error is obvious. Modernization and normalizing present no problems except for the French and bogus French; here the solution has been to preserve the mangled pronunciations when Madamoiselle is speaking English but to modernize the true French that she and Lady Fancyfull speak.

Since this was regarded as morally the most dubious of Restoration plays to survive through the eighteenth century, some alterations are almost part of its textual history. Vanbrugh himself rewrote two scenes; sententious speeches were interpolated into the text; and quite early it became custom to embellish the play with additional songs. The two of these which survive are given in Appendix A and the revised scenes in Appendix B; sententious interpolations will be discussed later in this introduction.

[1] The text is based on the copy of Q1 in the Lilly Library of Indiana University. A copy in the Newberry Library has also been collated; in seven instances the Lilly copy shows an obvious press correction when compared with the Newberry copy, but some twenty errors remain uncorrected. Copies of Q2 and P from the University of Washington Library and a copy of Q3 from the Newberry Library have been used in the collation.

[2] An edition marked "London. Printed in the year 1710" is, like the 1711 *Aesop*, printed for T. Johnson, Bookseller at The Hague. There is another Johnson edition in 1721. In each case the play was one of a series of English comedies for sale abroad, and obviously without textual authority.

Vanbrugh's true career as dramatist was brief. One season, 1696–1697, saw his only two original plays, *The Relapse* and *The Provoked Wife*, as well as *Aesop*, the first of his adaptations. He lived thirty years longer, translating freely, and leaving among his papers an incomplete original play, *A Journey to London*, which may have been written at any time in his career. Although at least one adaptation, *The Confederacy*, has considerable merit beyond what is found in its French original, Vanbrugh's reputation as dramatist must depend almost entirely on *The Relapse* and *The Provoked Wife*. There is enough similarity between these two that, had they been anonymous, we might conjecture that the same author wrote both; still, the differences between them are substantial, and these may be explained by circumstances of composition.

The Provoked Wife is said to have been begun while Vanbrugh was prisoner in the Bastille in 1692.[3] While this may be true, it was not to the stage that he looked upon his release, but rather to the army, and perhaps already to architecture. He probably wrote some dramatic bits and pieces during the next few years; otherwise the output of 1696–1697 would appear impossible. Colley Cibber's play *Love's Last Shift* acted as catalyst, moving Vanbrugh to rapid work for the theater. His "sequel" to Cibber's play, *The Relapse*, opened doors at both playhouses. For the old company at Drury Lane he followed *The Relapse* with *Aesop*, adapted from the French of Boursault, while for the rival company at Lincoln's Inn Fields he completed *The Provoked Wife*.

Examination of *The Provoked Wife* supports the conjecture that its composition was long drawn out, and that what was begun in too great leisure was finished in haste. It is a scene-by-scene play, not generously plotted, and with gratuitous scenes and set-piece dialogues to eke out its thin story. Its success lies in its premises, its characters, and dialogue in single scenes—not in development of action. A play too long in the making may well have these virtues and these defects. The central problem, the incompatible marriage, can be shown and can be discussed, but it cannot be resolved: Sir John and Lady Brute are in the same situation at the end of the play as at the beginning.

---

[3] Voltaire states (*Lettres philosophiques*, XIX) that Vanbrugh wrote a play in the Bastille, noting with surprise the absence of anti-French sentiment in it. He does not identify the play further. Since, on Cibber's testimony, it is clear that *The Provoked Wife* existed in some form before *The Relapse* was written, it is almost certain that it was Vanbrugh's Bastille play.

The other ingredients hardly affect the main plot: a female fop, a subsidiary pair of lovers, scenes of Sir John's debauchery, and occasional songs. Some devices, like the Rasor-Madamoiselle scene and Rasor's sudden, farcical repentance, may have been prompted by need to resolve the plot without adequate preparation.

The weak plotting scarcely matters. It may even be a virtue that the subordinate actions are too thin to distract interest from the main plot. It is surely a virtue that Vanbrugh refuses to evade the marriage problem by any kind of "happy" solution. Further, since the action is thin the characters have leisure to talk, and this play shows Vanbrugh's language at its best. He approaches Congreve in elegance and witty conversation, but his speech is more natural and less obviously contrived. One example must suffice, Heartfree's remark to Constant:

> Nay, I can court a woman too, call her nymph, angel, goddess,
> what you please; but here's the difference 'twixt you and I:
> I persuade a woman she's an angel; she persuades you she's one.
>
> (II.i.148–151)

This is worthy of Congreve, but one's first reaction is "how just', rather than "how elegant." The speech is so closely related to the characters that one cannot treat it as a detachable epigram. Such lines explain Cibber's praise:

> There is something so catching to the Ear, so easy to the Memory,
> in all he writ, that it has been observ'd by all the Actors of my
> Time, that the Style of no Author whatsoever gave their Memory
> less trouble than that of Sir *John Vanbrugh*.[4]

The play is everywhere rooted in theatrical tradition; scenes characters, and themes evoke associations with plays later than Van brugh's as well as earlier, and one cannot seek sources with any certainty. Still, Otway's *The Soldier's Fortune* (1681) stands close enough that it must be regarded as an influence, if not technically a source. At the center of Otway's play is the churlish, cowardly Sir Davy Dunce; Lady Dunce, making a confidante of her niece Sylvia, is quite explicit in declaring her dislike of Sir Davy and her interest in Captain Beaugard; a subsidiary action involving Sylvia and Beaugard's friend Courtine ends in marriage. The character grouping is exactly Vanbrugh's, and since the plots move along similar lines

---

[4] *An Apology for the Life of Colley Cibber*, ed. Robert W. Lowe (London, 1889), I, 219.

there is an occasional similarity in scenes. For subsidiary character interest, instead of Lady Fancyfull we have in Otway's play Sir Jolly Jumble, from whom Vanbrugh borrowed much to form Coupler in *The Relapse*. Otway's play is more elaborately plotted, and Lady Dunce is aggressive in pursuit of her lover in a way that Lady Brute could not be. There is what might be called a happy ending, when Sir Davy, threatened with blackmail, consents to countenance (and finance) a permanent liaison between Beaugard and Lady Dunce.

Behind *The Soldier's Fortune*, and also influencing Vanbrugh's play directly, lies Etherege's *She Would if She Could* (1668). Again there is the incompatible couple, Sir Oliver and Lady Cockwood. Sir Oliver's feeble attempts at debauchery, and also his cowardice, suggest Sir John Brute; his tavern companion Rakehell may have given part of his name to Lord Rake. But Lady Cockwood, far from being a suffering wife, is violent in her pursuit of Courtall, who unlike his counterparts in Otway and Vanbrugh is hard put to it to evade her advances.

Sir Oliver Cockwood, Sir Davy Dunce, Sir John Brute—even the knight's title in Restoration comedy can warn against a character. The earliest were knights of Cromwell's creation, like Etherege's Sir Nicholas Cully. Slightly later, Sir Oliver Cockwood, although a country knight, has a suggestive given name. Sir Davy Dunce presumably was, like Sir John Brute, knighted by the king, but the former association still lingers. One is apt to expect debauchery, cowardice, stupidity, sometimes even specifically Puritan vices like hypocrisy and greed from these knights.[5] They profess to be libertines, but their debauches are puny compared to those of actual rakes like Sir Charles Sedley or the Earl of Rochester. Sir John simply has not the ability to lead the libertine life:

SIR JOHN.
> Why did I marry? I married because I had a mind to lie
> with her, and she would not let me.

HEARTFREE.
> Why did you not ravish her?

[5] Knights (or baronets—one cannot always distinguish) are sometimes mere gulls or eccentrics, like Wycherley's Sir Simon Addleplot or Shadwell's Sir Nicholas Gimcrack. Alternatively they are fops like Sir Fopling Flutter, Sir Courtly Nice, or Sir Novelty Fashion. Sensible elderly knights like Shadwell's Sir Edward Belfond are rare; Etherege's Sir Frederick Frollick is almost unique as hero and gentleman—and for him both terms need qualification.

SIR JOHN.

Yes, and so have hedged myself into forty quarrels with her relations, besides buying my pardon. But more than all that, you must know I was afraid of being damned in those days, for I kept sneaking cowardly company, fellows that went to church, said grace to their meat, and had not the least tincture of quality about 'em.   (II.i.257–262).

Sir John is responsible for the failure of his marriage, and his intractable nature is Vanbrugh's evidence for the hopelessness of some marriages. Many Restoration plays beyond those so far mentioned present mismatches—old and young, puritan and libertine, foolish and sensible—and all might have given hints for *The Provoked Wife*. Before going further, one must distinguish a rather different kind of play—one that attacks marriage as an institution, doomed even though the partners are sensible. Typical of these plays is Dryden's *Marriage à la Mode* (1672), where a young and witty couple soon fall into boredom. Asked whether his wife is beautiful, the husband can only answer, "Ask those who have smelt to a strong perfume two years together, what's the scent," and summarizes the story of his marriage, "At last we arrived at that point, that there was nothing left in us to make us new to one another." Dryden's couple shows us what Congreve's young lovers (and Heartfree and Bellinda in our present play) feared. Such fears make for wit combats and other techniques we associate with the comedy of manners; Sir John and Lady Brute are too far mismatched for such elegant sparring, and that may be a reason we think Vanbrugh less representative of the highest comedy of manners than Etherege or Congreve. We must recognize the world of difference between Vanbrugh's treatment of a mismatch and Dryden's indictment of all marriage.

In any case, what solution? There was, for all practical purposes, no divorce procedure. The simplest way of handling an unsuccessful marriage would be separation by mutual consent; the agreement would not come under cognizance of law at all, and of course neither party could remarry. In more formal procedure, an injured party could bring suit for separation in an ecclesiastical court. The only effective ground was adultery—by one party only, proven by more than mere confession, and free from any suspicion of collusion. The proceedings necessarily brought scandal and they were long drawn-out. Such a separation did not allow either party to remarry, and the husband—even if he were the injured party—was forced to provide a separate maintenance for the wife. This idea, however, did cross Sir John's mind: "If I could but catch her adulterating I might be divorced from her by law." Heartfree makes the obvious response: "And so pay her a yearly pension to be a distinguished cuckold" (III.i.101–104).

The situation was to change, if only slightly, almost at the time of the play, when the possibility arose of a parliamentary divorce with permission to remarry. This procedure was stabilized early in the next century: the husband first obtained a separation in the ecclesiastical court, next won damages by suing the adulterer for criminal conversation, and only then could ask for an act in parliament. Since this procedure had not yet developed (the first parliamentary divorce was granted in the year following the play), Vanbrugh's references to divorce are vague. Lady Brute can speak of a court of chancery in heaven that would free her, and she and Bellinda speak of a House of Lords in which she would infallibly carry her cause (I.i.95–98). In heaven perhaps; but on earth no woman was granted a parliamentary divorce until the nineteenth century.[6]

Perhaps Lady Brute did not understand matrimonial law fully, but Vanbrugh understood enough to know that neither church nor state provided remedy, and that solutions proposed on stage hardly applied to real life. Actually, most plays contented themselves with amusement at the mismatched couple, for whom casual and comic adultery was an outlet of sorts. Congreve's first three comedies had contained such scenes (with women as aggressors in the first two), and Vanbrugh's own *Relapse* combined a serious view of marriage with the most joyous of off-stage seductions. Such illustrations are legion, but there are few scenes in which a playwright looks to practical action following a recognition of marital incompatibility. In *Marriage à la Mode* Dryden's couple is led back to dubious monogamy because each partner realizes that he has a rival and hence that there must be something attractive about the other. *The Soldier's Fortune* ends in a permanent liaison with the husband permanently dispossessed. A play not so far mentioned, Southerne's *The Wives' Excuse* (December, 1691), is important in the development of the divorce theme in comedy, though it was a failure on the stage and does not appear to have influenced Vanbrugh. It ends with a separation by agreement, but

---

6 The definitive work on this subject is Gellert Spencer Alleman, *Matrimonial Law and Restoration Comedy* (Philadelphia, 1942), pp. 106–141.

with very little detail as to financial arrangements or the future status of the released wife. For such things we must look to a later play, Farquhar's *The Beaux' Stratagem* (1707), where Squire and Mrs. Sullen, prompted by her brother, agree to separate. They improvise what is almost a marriage ceremony in reverse. The more substantial problem of the return of Mrs. Sullen's fortune is solved by a convenient robbery that puts Sullen's papers into the hands of his brother-in-law. The final problem, Mrs. Sullen's fate, will presumably be solved by her union with her lover. Farquhar pleads eloquently for the dissolution of marriage,[7] and he ignores legal realities to such an extent that later readers have assumed that this divorce was actual and possible, and do not realize that Farquhar's ending was a comedy of evasions.[8]

Lady Dunce in a play of 1681 and Mrs. Sullen in one of 1707 both find a solution in adultery. There is a difference between Otway's open immorality and Farquhar's theatrical solution a quarter of a century later, though it might take a casuist to define it. For Vanbrugh, midway between these dates, neither immorality nor sentimentality could solve Lady Brute's problem. To illustrate from his own characters in *The Relapse*: a widow like Berinthia and a husband like Loveless might enjoy sexual freedom, but a wife-heroine like Amanda remained virtuous, no matter how great the temptation or how near she might come to yielding. So Lady Brute; and those who imagine a sixth act to the play in which she yields to Constant are probably undervaluing the firm moral structure behind the loose talk of the play.[9]

In 1695, after a thirteen-year monopoly, London again had two theatrical companies when Betterton and others broke away from the United Company at Drury Lane. Vanbrugh's early relationship with the two companies is not quite clear. Since his first play, *The Relapse*, was a sequel to a Drury Lane play it naturally went there. So did *Aesop*. There was also an *Aesop*, Part II, first acted at Drury Lane in the spring of 1697, which contained a scene of theater propaganda in

---

7 It has even been argued that Farquhar drew on Milton's work: Martin A. Larson, "The Influence of Milton's Divorce Tracts on Farquhar's *Beaux Strategem*," *PMLA*, XXXIX (1924), 174–178.

8 See Alleman, pp. 106, 112.

9 The best discussion of Vanbrugh's moral views is still Paul Mueschke and Jeannette Fleisher, "A Re-Evaluation of Vanbrugh," *PMLA*, XLIX (1934), 848–889.

which Aesop persuades the Betterton group that they have no real grievance and should return to the parent company. But at the very time this scene was being prepared, Vanbrugh was finishing *The Provoked Wife* for Betterton's company. There is no clear reason for this change of allegiance in the middle of an extraordinary first season. Perhaps, as one who did not wish to be regarded as a professional playwright, Vanbrugh felt that he should not favor either playhouse over the other. (He seems to have given his benefits from *The Provoked Wife* to the actors, if the epilogue is to be taken literally.) And there may be something to Cibber's story that the Earl of Halifax, who had heard the play read to him at an earlier time, persuaded Vanbrugh to revise it and give it to the Betterton company.[10] In any case, the play was first acted by that company at Lincoln's Inn Fields in the spring of 1697 (probably April), and from then on Vanbrugh's fortunes were joined with theirs, even to the extent of building the Queen's Theatre in the Haymarket for them and sharing in the management—disasters both.

The immediate consequence of this change of companies was a cast far beyond what Drury Lane could provide—above all, Betterton himself, and Mrs. Barry and Mrs. Bracegirdle as Lady Brute and Bellinda. The company did not advertise regularly until the 1705–1706 season; we are dependent on inference for early stage history, but everything suggests an instant and continued success for the play. A second edition was called for in 1698; St. Evremond translated it into French; it was denounced by Jeremy Collier in 1698, and in 1701 its actors were indicted for profane language on the stage; in a work of theatrical gossip, *A Comparison Between the Two Stages* (1702), it is mentioned as a play that sustained Betterton's company in its competition. When records begin again in 1706 we find the old cast almost intact. After Betterton, Keene took the part of Sir John, then in 1719 Quin. The play remained exclusively in the Lincoln's Inn Fields repertory until 1726, performances gradually becoming less frequent. Then came the Drury Lane production of January, 1726, with Cibber as Sir John and the two raucous new scenes involving Sir John in woman's clothes. Lincoln's Inn Fields countered with its embellished production in March, and the competition obviously increased the play's popularity.

Since this was the most consistently popular Restoration play on the eighteenth-century stage, it is impossible to give its history in

10 Cibber, I, 217.

detail. Garrick first played Sir John in 1744; on occasion Macklin took the part, and Quin remained as rival to both. Toward the end of the century the popularity of the play waned: there were moral problems; other plays of its period had long vanished; and the succession of great character actors to play Sir John had ended. It is with reference to Sir John that the stage history must be discussed, even though there are six fine roles in the play as well as specialty parts for Rasor and Madamoiselle. As for the actresses, we can only note that Anne Oldfield, since she was at Drury Lane, had no opportunity to play Lady Brute until 1726; Susanna Cibber and Peg Woffington were among the most important of her successors. And any stage history should mention the prominence of John Beard and other singers who took the part of Colonel Bully.

Since in Vanbrugh's play Colonel Bully has practically no lines, this prominence should be a warning that changes were taking place in the eighteenth-century productions. Even the original play was embellished with songs, and a number of early notices advise us of special features: "with alterations" (1706); "a new epilogue spoken by Mrs. Cross" (1716); "with a new prologue" (1717); "singing by Leveridge, 'The Tippling Philosophers' " (1720). After the Drury Lane production of 1726 such embellishments are usually noted in advertisements.

More important was what was not advertised, the softening and expurgation of the text. The practice in late eighteenth-century play-books of either making cuts or indicating them by setting passages off by quotation marks enables us to see part of the process. These texts also give new speeches meant to destroy the hardness that is Vanbrugh's peculiar excellence. Lady Brute's soliloquy in the first scene, which Vanbrugh ended with a defiant "Virtue's an ass, and a gallant's worth forty on't" (I.i.77–78), is cut back to its first half, and ends:

> But hold. Let me go no further. I think I have a right to alarm this surly brute of mine, but if I know my heart, it will never let me go so far as to injure him.[11]

[11] This and the following two passages are quoted from the edition of 1776, "Marked with variations in the Manager's Book," printed for J. Rivington, etc. In this edition Lady Brute's original speech continues through her line, "Perhaps a good part of what I suffer from my husband may be a judgment upon me for my cruelty to my lover" (I.i.62), before moving to the new conclusion. In later theatrical collections her lines are even more sharply cut.

Nothing can quite redeem Sir John, but he is given a speech in answer to Bellinda's last line, closing the play with—

> Surly I may be, stubborn I am not,
> For I have both forgiven and forgot.
> If so, be these our judges, Mrs. Pert,
> 'Tis more by my goodness than your desert.[12]

But not all additions serve morality; actors' interpolations are apt to do the reverse. One such interpolation is the broken-rhyme couplet with which Rasor concludes Act V, scene ii, just before carrying off the drunken Sir John:

> My master's asleep in his chair and a-snoring,
> My lady's abroad, and—oh, rare matrimony![13]

The nineteenth-century stage history of the play is a blank, though it appears frequently enough in collections to show that it had not been entirely forgotten. It would be pleasant to report that in the present century it had come into its own again. It has not. The Stage Society performed it in London in 1919; a summer performance at the Vaudeville (London) in 1963 was probably the most notable performance in a century and a half. Undoubtedly there have been productions elsewhere. Still, the disappearance of this most durable of Restoration plays when others are revived (even its quasi-source, *The Soldier's Fortune*, has had two productions in London's West End) asks explanation. Perhaps the play is too good: it will not allow a theatrical happy ending to solve the insoluble, and will not subordinate theme and character to plot.

CURT A. ZIMANSKY

University of Iowa

---

12 The last couplet is difficult. Some later editions (e.g., Mrs. Inchbald's *British Theatre*, London, 1808) quite change its meaning by inserting a half-line, "If they approve" just before the final line.

13 These lines appear even in Mrs. Inchbald's chaste edition. In general, the process of deterioration of the acting text was first by cutting, only later by additions to the dialogue. Garrick's promptbook, a marked copy of the Dublin 1743 edition, shows almost no additions but more than 75 omissions; it is extensively described in Kalman A. Burnim, *David Garrick, Director* (Pittsburgh, 1961), pp. 174–188.

THE PROVOKED WIFE

PROLOGUE

Spoken by Mrs. Bracegirdle

Since 'tis the intent and business of the stage
To copy out the follies of the age,
To hold to every man a faithful glass
And show him of what species he's an ass,
I hope the next that teaches in the school   5
Will show our author he's a scribbling fool.
And that the satire may be sure to bite,
Kind heaven, inspire some venomed priest to write,
And grant some ugly lady may indite.
For I would have him lashed, by heavens! I would,   10
Till his presumption swam away in blood.
Three plays at once proclaims a face of brass,
No matter what they are. That's not the case;
To write three plays, even that's to be an ass.
But what I least forgive, he knows it too,   15
For to his cost he lately has known you.
Experience shows, to many a writer's smart,
You hold a court where mercy ne'er had part;
So much of the old serpent's sting you have,
You love to damn, as heaven delights to save.   20
In foreign parts let a bold volunteer
For public good upon the stage appear,
He meets ten thousand smiles to dissipate his fear.
All tickle on th'adventuring young beginner,
And only scourge th'incorrigible sinner;   25
They touch indeed his faults, but with a hand
So gentle, that his merit still may stand;
Kindly they buoy the follies of his pen,
That he may shun 'em when he writes again.
But 'tis not so in this good-natured town,   30
All's one, an ox, a poet, or a crown,
Old England's play was always knocking down.

---

14. even] *Q1–2* (ev'n); e'en *Q3, P.*   24. th'] *Q1–2*; the *Q3, P.*

8. *venomed priest*] This wish was granted a year later with the publication of Jeremy Collier's *Short View of the Immorality and Profaneness of the English Stage*, which attacked Vanbrugh with special severity.

12. *Three . . . once*] Earlier in the 1696–1697 season, Vanbrugh's *The Relapse* and *Aesop* had been staged.

DRAMATIS PERSONAE

CONSTANT	Mr. Verbruggen	
HEARTFREE	Mr. Hudson	
SIR JOHN BRUTE	Mr. Betterton	
TREBLE, a singing master	Mr. Bowman	
RASOR, valet de chambre to Sir John Brute	Mr. Bowen	5
JUSTICE OF THE PEACE	Mr. Bright	
LORD RAKE ⎫ companions to Sir John Brute COLONEL BULLY ⎭		
CONSTABLE AND WATCH		10
LADY BRUTE	Mrs. Barry	
BELLINDA, her niece	Mrs. Bracegirdle	
LADY FANCYFULL	Mrs. Bowman	
MADAMOISELLE	Mrs. Willis	
CORNET AND PIPE, servants to Lady Fancyfull		15

---

14. *Madamoiselle*] This is the spelling in all early editions.
15. To the cast should be added: a Justice; Lovewell, serving woman to Lady Brute; Jo, a porter; footmen, servants, and pages.

The Provoked Wife
A Comedy

ACT I

Sir John Brute's House.
Enter Sir John, *solus.*

SIR JOHN.

What cloying meat is love, when matrimony's the sauce to
it. Two years' marriage has debauched my five senses.
Everything I see, everything I hear, everything I feel,
everything I smell, and everything I taste—methinks has
wife in't. No boy was ever so weary of his tutor, no girl of   5
her bib, no nun of doing penance, nor old maid of being
chaste, as I am of being married. Sure there's a secret curse
entailed upon the very name of wife. My lady is a young
lady, a fine lady, a witty lady, a virtuous lady—and yet I
hate her. There is but one thing on earth I loathe beyond   10
her; that's fighting. Would my courage come up but to a
fourth part of my ill nature, I'd stand buff to her relations
and thrust her out of doors. But marriage has sunk me down
to such an ebb of resolution, I dare not draw my sword,
though even to get rid of my wife. But here she comes.   15

Enter Lady Brute.

LADY BRUTE.

Do you dine at home today, Sir John?

SIR JOHN.

Why, do you expect I should tell you what I don't know
myself?

LADY BRUTE.

I thought there was no harm in asking you.

6. nor] *Q1–3*; or *P.*

---

12. *stand buff*] stand firm.

SIR JOHN.

> If thinking wrong were an excuse for impertinence, women   20
> might be justified in most things they say or do.

LADY BRUTE.

> I'm sorry I have said anything to displease you.

SIR JOHN.

> Sorrow for things past is of as little importance to me as my
> dining at home or abroad ought to be to you.

LADY BRUTE.

> My inquiry was only that I might have provided what you   25
> liked.

SIR JOHN.

> Six to four you had been in the wrong there again, for what
> I liked yesterday I don't like today, and what I like today
> 'tis odds I mayn't like tomorrow.

LADY BRUTE.

> But if I had asked you what you liked?   30

SIR JOHN.

> Why then there would have been more asking about it than
> the thing was worth.

LADY BRUTE.

> I wish I did but know how I might please you.

SIR JOHN.

> Aye, but that sort of knowledge is not a wife's talent.

LADY BRUTE.

> Whate'er my talent is, I'm sure my will has ever been to   35
> make you easy.

SIR JOHN.

> If women were to have their wills, the world would be
> finely governed.

LADY BRUTE.

> What reason have I given you to use me as you do of late?
> It once was otherwise; you married me for love.   40

SIR JOHN.

> And you me for money; so you have your reward and I have
> mine.

LADY BRUTE.

> What is it that disturbs you?

22 I have] *Q1–2*; I've *Q3, P.*   32 was] *Q1–3*; is *P.*

SIR JOHN.
  A parson.
LADY BRUTE.
  Why, what has he done to you?   45
SIR JOHN.
  He has married me.   *Exit* Sir John.
LADY BRUTE (*sola*).
  The devil's in the fellow, I think. I was told before I married
  him that thus 'twould be. But I thought I had charms
  enough to govern him, and that where there was an estate a
  woman must needs be happy; so my vanity has deceived   50
  me and my ambition has made me uneasy. But some
  comfort still: if one would be revenged of him, these are
  good times. A woman may have a gallant and a separate
  maintenance too. The surly puppy! Yet he's a fool for't.
  For hitherto he has been no monster, but who knows how   55
  far he may provoke me. I never loved him, yet I have been
  ever true to him, and that in spite of all the attacks of art
  and nature upon a poor weak woman's heart in favor of a
  tempting lover. Methinks so noble a defense as I have made
  should be rewarded with a better usage. Or who can tell?   60
  Perhaps a good part of what I suffer from my husband may
  be a judgment upon me for my cruelty to my lover. Lord,
  with what pleasure could I indulge that thought, were there
  but a possibility of finding arguments to make it good. And
  how do I know but there may? Let me see. What opposes?   65
  My matrimonial vow? Why, what did I vow? I think I
  promised to be true to my husband. Well; and he promised
  to be kind to me. But he han't kept his word. Why then
  I'm absolved from mine. Aye, that seems clear to me. The
  argument's good between the king and the people, why not   70
  between the husband and the wife? O, but that condition
  was not expressed. No matter, 'twas understood. Well, by all
  I see, if I argue the matter a little longer with myself, I

53–54. *a gallant . . . maintenance*] A woman divorced for adultery was still
entitled to a separate maintenance from her husband.

55. *monster*] cuckold.

70. *argument's . . . people*] Lady Brute echoes the social contract theory
popularized by the revolution of 1688: if the king fails to fulfill his promises,
the people are released from theirs.

shan't find so many bugbears in the way as I thought I
should. Lord, what fine notions of virtue do we women take   75
up upon the credit of old foolish philosophers. Virtue's its
own reward, virtue's this, virtue's that. Virtue's an ass, and
a gallant's worth forty on't.

Enter Bellinda.

Good morrow, dear cousin.

BELLINDA.

Good morrow, madam; you look pleased this morning.   80

LADY BRUTE.

I am so.

BELLINDA.

With what, pray?

LADY BRUTE.

With my husband.

BELLINDA.

Drown husbands, for yours is a provoking fellow. As he went
out just now I prayed him to tell me what time of day 'twas,   85
and he asked me if I took him for the church clock, that was
obliged to tell all the parish.

LADY BRUTE.

He has been saying some good obliging things to me, too.
In short, Bellinda, he has used me so barbarously of late
that I could almost resolve to play the downright wife—and   90
cuckold him.

BELLINDA.

That would be downright indeed.

LADY BRUTE.

Why, after all, there's more to be said for't than you'd
imagine, child. I know according to the strict statute law of
religion I should do wrong, but if there were a Court of   95
Chancery in heaven I'm sure I should cast him.

BELLINDA.

If there were a House of Lords you might.

95–96. *Court of Chancery*] a court of equity to provide justice when there
was no form of action at law that could bring relief. But on earth Chancery
did not deal with divorce.

97. *House of Lords*] an imprecise reference to some form of parliamentary
action. See Introduction, p. xviii.

LADY BRUTE.

In either I should infallibly carry my cause. Why, he is the
first aggressor, not I.

BELLINDA.

Aye, but you know, we must return good for evil.   100

LADY BRUTE.

That may be a mistake in the translation. Prithee be of my
opinion, Bellinda, for I'm positive I'm in the right; and if
you'll keep up the prerogative of a woman, you'll likewise
be positive you are in the right whenever you do anything
you have a mind to. But I shall play the fool, and jest on till   105
I make you begin to think I'm in earnest.

BELLINDA.

I shan't take the liberty, madam, to think of anything that
you desire to keep a secret from me.

LADY BRUTE.

Alas, my dear, I have no secrets. My heart could never yet
confine my tongue.   110

LELLINDA.

Your eyes, you mean, for I am sure I have seen them
gadding when your tongue has been locked up safe enough.

BADY BRUTE.

My eyes gadding? Prithee after who, child?

BELLINDA.

Why, after one that thinks you hate him, as much as I know
you love him.   115

LADY BRUTE.

Constant, you mean.

BELLINDA.

I do so.

LADY BRUTE.

Lord, what should put such a thing into your head?

BELLINDA.

That which puts things into most people's heads, observa-
tion.   12

LADY BRUTE.

Why, what have you observed, in the name of wonder?

BELLINDA.

I have observed you blush when you meet him, force

122. meet] *Q1–3*; met *P.*

yourself away from him, and then be out of humor with
everything about you. In a word, never was poor creature
so spurred on by desire and so reined in with fear.   125

LADY BRUTE.
How strong is fancy!

BELLINDA.
How weak is woman.

LADY BRUTE.
Prithee, niece, have a better opinion of your aunt's inclinations.

BELLINDA.
Dear aunt, have a better opinion of your niece's under-   130
standing.

LADY BRUTE.
You'll make me angry.

BELLINDA.
You'll make me laugh.

LADY BRUTE.
Then you are resolved to persist?

BELLINDA.
Positively.   135

LADY BRUTE.
And all I can say—

BELLINDA.
Will signify nothing.

LADY BRUTE.
Though I should swear 'twere false—

BELLINDA.
I should think it true.

LADY BRUTE.
Then let us both forgive (*kissing her*), for we have both 140
offended, I in making a secret, you in discovering it.

BELLINDA.
Good nature may do much. But you have more reason to
forgive one, than I have to pardon t'other.

LADY BRUTE.
'Tis true, Bellinda, you have given me so many proofs of

128–129. inclinations] *Q1–2*; inclination *Q3, P.*

your friendship that my reserve has been indeed a crime. 145
But that you may more easily forgive me, remember, child,
that when our nature prompts us to a thing our honor and
religion have forbid us, we would (were't possible) conceal
even from the soul itself the knowledge of the body's
weakness.   150

BELLINDA.

Well, I hope, to make your friend amends, you'll hide
nothing from her for the future, though the body should
still grow weaker and weaker.

LADY BRUTE.

No, from this moment I have no more reserve; and for a
proof of my repentance, I own, Bellinda, I'm in danger. 155
Merit and wit assault me from without, nature and love
solicit me within, my husband's barbarous usage piques me
to revenge, and Satan catching at the fair occasion throws
in my way that vengeance which of all vengeance pleases
women best.   160

BELLINDA.

'Tis well Constant don't know the weakness of the fortifica-
tions, for o' my conscience he'd soon come on to the assault.

LADY BRUTE.

Aye, and I'm afraid carry the town too. But whatever you
may have observed, I have dissembled so well as to keep
him ignorant. So you see I'm no coquette, Bellinda; and if 165
you'll follow my advice you'll never be one neither. 'Tis true,
coquetry is one of the main ingredients in the natural composition of a woman, and I as well as others could be well
enough pleased to see a crowd of young fellows ogling
and glancing and watching all occasions to do forty foolish 170
officious things, nay, should some of 'em push on, even to
hanging or drowning. Why, faith, if I should let pure
woman alone, I should e'en be but too well pleased with't.

BELLINDA.

I'll swear 'twould tickle me strangely.

LADY BRUTE.

But, after all, 'tis a vicious practice in us to give the 175
least encouragement but where we design to come to a

166. you'll follow] Q 1–3; you follow
P.

conclusion. For 'tis an unreasonable thing to engage a man
in a disease which we beforehand resolve we never will apply
a cure to.

BELLINDA.

'Tis true; but then a woman must abandon one of the su- 180
preme blessings of her life. For I am fully convinced, no man
has half that pleasure in possessing a mistress as a woman
has in jilting a gallant.

LADY BRUTE.

The happiest woman then on earth must be our neighbor.

BELLINDA.

O the impertinent composition! She has vanity and affec- 185
tation enough to make her a ridiculous original in spite of
all that art and nature ever furnished to any of her sex before
her.

LADY BRUTE.

She concludes all men her captives, and whatever course
they take it serves to confirm her in that opinion. 190

BELLINDA.

If they shun her, she thinks 'tis modesty and takes it for a
proof of their passion.

LADY BRUTE.

And if they are rude to her, 'tis conduct and done to prevent
town talk.

BELLINDA.

When her folly makes 'em laugh, she thinks they are 195
pleased with her wit.

LADY BRUTE.

And when her impertinence makes 'em dull, concludes they
are jealous of her favors.

BELLINDA.

All their actions and their words, she takes for granted, aim
at her. 200

LADY BRUTE.

And pities all other women, because she thinks they envy
her.

BELLINDA.

Pray, out of pity to ourselves let us find a better subject, for

---

186. *original*] eccentric person.

I am weary of this. Do you think your husband inclined to
jealousy?   205

LADY BRUTE.

O no, he does not love me well enough for that. Lord, how
wrong men's maxims are. They are seldom jealous of their
wives unless they are very fond of 'em, whereas they ought to
consider the woman's inclinations, for there depends their
fate. Well, men may talk, but they are not so wise as we, 210
that's certain.

BELLINDA.

At least in our affairs.

LADY BRUTE.

Nay, I believe we should outdo 'em in the business of the
state, too; for methinks they do and undo, and make but
mad work on't.   215

BELLINDA.

Why then don't we get into the intrigues of government as
well as they?

LADY BRUTE.

Because we have intrigues of our own that make us more
sport, child. And so let's in and consider of 'em.   *Exeunt.*

[I.ii]   *A dressing room.*
         Enter Lady Fancyfull, Madamoiselle, *and* Cornet.

LADY FANCYFULL.

How do I look this morning?

CORNET.

Your ladyship looks very ill, truly.

LADY FANCYFULL.

Lard, how ill-natured thou art, Cornet, to tell me so, though
the thing should be true. Don't you know that I have
humility enough to be but too easily out of conceit with   5
myself? Hold the glass; I dare swear that will have more
manners than you have. Madamoiselle, let me have your
opinion too.

209. woman's] *Q1*; women's *Q2–3*,   214. mad] *Q1*; bad *Q2–3, P.*
P.

MADAMOISELLE.

My opinion pe, matam, dat your ladyship never look so well
in your life.   10

LADY FANCYFULL.

Well, the French are the prettiest obliging people, they say
the most acceptable, well-mannered things—and never
flatter.

MADAMOISELLE.

Your ladyship say great justice inteed.

LADY FANCYFULL.

Nay, everything's just in my house but Cornet. The very   15
looking glass gives her the *dementi*. But I'm almost afraid it
flatters me, it makes me look so very engaging.

Looking affectedly in the glass.

MADAMOISELLE.

Inteed, matam, your face pe hansomer den all de looking
glass in te world, *croyez moi*.

LADY FANCYFULL.

But is it possible my eyes can be so languishing, and so very   20
full of fire?

MADAMOISELLE.

Matam, if de glass was burning glass, I believe your eyes
set de fire in de house.

LADY FANCYFULL.

You may take that nightgown, Madamoiselle. Get out of
the room, Cornet, I can't endure you. This wench methinks   25
does look so unsufferably ugly.   *Exit* Cornet.

MADAMOISELLE.

Everting look ugly, matam, dat stand by your latyship.

LADY FANCYFULL.

No, really, Madamoiselle, methinks you look mighty pretty.

MADAMOISELLE.

Ah, matam, de moon have no eclat ven de sun appear.

LADY FANCYFULL.

O pretty expression! Have you ever been in love Madam-   30
oiselle?

26. S.D. *Exit* Cornet] *Q1*; *omit*
Q2–3, P.

_____

16. *the dementi*] the lie.
19. *croyez moi*] believe me.

MADAMOISELLE (*sighing*).

Oui, matam.

LADY FANCYFULL.

And were you beloved again?

MADAMOISELLE (*sighing*).

No, matam.

LADY FANCYFULL.

O ye gods, what an unfortunate creature should I be in such   35
a case. But nature has made me nice for my own defense.
I'm nice, strangely nice, Madamoiselle. I believe were the
merit of whole mankind bestowed upon one single person,
I should still think the fellow wanted something to make it
worth my while to take notice of him. And yet I could love,   40
nay fondly love, were it possible to have a thing made on
purpose for me; for I'm not cruel, Madamoiselle, I'm only
nice.

MADAMOISELLE.

Ah, matam, I wish I was fine gentelman for your sake.
I do all de ting in de world to get leetel way into your   45
heart. I make song, I make verse, I give you de serenade,
I give great many present to Madamoiselle. I no eat, I no
sleep, I be lean, I be mad, I hang myself, I drown myself.
Ah ma chère dame, que je vous aimerais.   *Embracing her.*

LADY FANCYFULL.

Well, the French have strange, obliging ways with 'em.   50
You may take those two pair of gloves, Madamoiselle.

MADAMOISELLE.

Me humbly tanke my sweet lady.

Enter Cornet.

CORNET.

Madam, here's a letter for your ladyship by the penny post.

LADY FANCYFULL.

Some new conquest, I'll warrant you. For, without vanity,
I looked extremely clear last night when I went to the Park.   55
O, agreeable! Here's a new song made of me. And ready
set too. O thou welcome thing. (*Kissing it.*)   Call Pipe
hither, she shall sing it instantly.

---

49. *Ah . . . aimerais*] Ah my dear lady, how I would love you.
55. *Park*] St. James's Park, the fashionable promenade.

Enter Pipe.

Here, sing me this new song, Pipe.

SONG

I.

[PIPE.]   Fly, fly, you happy shepherds, fly,   60
        Avoid Philira's charms;
        The rigor of her heart denies
          The heaven that's in her arms.
        Ne'er hope to gaze and then retire,
          Nor yielding, to be blest;   65
        Nature who formed her eyes of fire,
          Of ice composed her breast.

II.

        Yet, lovely maid, this once believe
          A slave, whose zeal you move.
        The gods, alas, your youth deceive;   70
          Their heaven consists in love.
        In spite of all the thanks you owe,
          You may reproach 'em this,
        That where they did their form bestow
          They have denied their bliss. [*Exit* Pipe.] 75

LADY FANCYFULL.

Well, there may be faults, Madamoiselle, but the design is so
very obliging, 'twould be a matchless ingratitude in me to
discover 'em.

MADAMOISELLE.

Ma foi, matam, I tink de gentelman's song tell you de trute.
If you never love, you never be happy. *Ah, que j'aime* 80
l'amour, moi.

Enter Servant *with another letter.*

SERVANT.

Madam, here's another letter for your ladyship.   [*Exit.*]

71. Their] *Q1, P*; The *Q2–3*.   80. j'aime] *Q1–2* (I'aime); *l'aime*
                                        Q2–3, P.

80–81. *Ah . . . moi*] Ah, how I am in love with love.

LADY FANCYFULL.

'Tis thus I am importuned every morning, Madamoiselle.
Pray, how do the French ladies when they are thus
accablées?   85

MADAMOISELLE.

Matam, dey never complain. *Au contraire*. When one Frense
laty have got hundred lover, den she do all she can—to get
hundred more.

LADY FANCYFULL.

Well, strike me dead, I think they have *le goût bon*. For 'tis an
unutterable pleasure to be adored by all the men and envied   90
by all the women. Yet I'll swear I'm concerned at the
torture I give 'em. Lard, why was I formed to make the
whole creation uneasy? But let me read my letter. (*Reads*).
"If you have a mind to hear of your faults instead of being
praised for your virtues, take the pains to walk in the Green   95
Walk in St. James's with your woman an hour hence.
You'll there meet one who hates you for some things as he
could love you for others, and therefore is willing to endeavor your reformation. If you come to the place I mention, you'll know who I am; if you don't, you never shall, so 100
take your choice." This is strangely familiar, Madamoiselle.
Now have I a provoking fancy to know who this impudent
fellow is.

MADAMOISELLE.

Den take your scarf and your mask and go to de rendezvous.
De Frense laty do *justement comme ça*.   105

LADY FANCYFULL.

Rendezvous! What, rendezvous with a man, Madamoiselle?

MADAMOISELLE.

Eh, pourquoi non?

LADY FANCYFULL.

What, and a man perhaps I never saw in my life?

MADAMOISELLE.

Tant mieux, c'est donc quelque chose de nouveau.

---

85. *accablées*] overburdened.
86. *Au contraire*] on the contrary.   89. *le goût bon*] good taste.
105. *justement comme ça*] just like that.
107. *Eh, pourquoi non?*] Well, why not?
109. *Tant . . . nouveau*] So much the better, then it will be something new.

LADY FANCYFULL.

    Why, how do I know what designs he may have? He may 110
intend to ravish me for aught I know.

MADAMOISELLE.

    Ravish? Bagatelle. I would fain see one impudent rogue
ravish madamoiselle; *oui, je le voudrais.*

LADY FANCYFULL.

    O but my reputation, Madamoiselle, my reputation. *Ah ma
chère réputation.* 115

MADAMOISELLE.

    Matam, *quand on l'a une fois perdue, on n'en est plus embarrassée.*

LADY FANCYFULL.

    Fe, Madamoiselle, fe! Reputation is a jewel.

MADAMOISELLE.

    Que coûte bien chère, matam.

LADY FANCYFULL.

    Why sure you would not sacrifice your honor to your
pleasure? 120

MADAMOISELLE.

    Je suis philosophe.

LADY FANCYFULL.

    Bless me how your talk. Why, what if honor be a burden,
Madamoiselle, must it not be borne?

MADAMOISELLE.

    *Chaqu'un à sa façon. Quand quelque chose m'incommode, moi, je
m'en défais, vite.* 125

LADY FANCYFULL.

    Get you gone, you little naughty French woman you, I vow
and swear I must turn you out of doors if you talk thus.

MADAMOISELLE.

    Turn me out of doors? Turn yourself out of doors and go
see what de gentelman have to say to you. *Tenez!* (*Giving*

---

    113. *oui, je le voudrais*] yes, I would.

    114–116. *Ah . . . embarrassée*] "Ah, my dear reputation." "Madam, when one has once lost it, one is no longer embarrassed by it."

    118. *Que . . . chère*] Which costs a great deal.

    121. *Je suis philosophe*] I am philosophical.

    124–125. *Chaqu'un . . . vite*] Each in his own way. Whenever something inconveniences me, I get rid of it quickly.

    129—131. *Tenez . . . tout*] Stop! Here is your scarf, here your headpiece, here your mask—everything.

her her things hastily.) *Voilà votre écharpe, voilà votre coiffe, voilà* 130
votre masque, voilà tout! (*Calling within.*) Hey, Mercure,
Coquin, call one chair for matam and one oder for me, *va*
t'en vite! (*Turning to her lady and helping her on hastily with her*
things.) *Allons,* matam, *dépêchez-vous donc. Mon dieu, quelles*
scrupules!   135

LADY FANCYFULL.
   Well, for once, Madamoiselle, I'll follow your advice, out
   of the intemperate desire I have to know who this ill-bred
   fellow is. But I have too much delicatesse to make a practice
   on it.

MADAMOISELLE.
   Belle chose vraiment que la delicatesse, lorsqu'il s'agit de se 140
   divertir. À ça, vous voilà équipée, partons! He bien, qu'avez-vous
   donc?

LADY FANCYFULL.
   J'ai peur.

MADAMOISELLE.
   Je n'en ai point, moi.

LADY FANCYFULL.
   I dare not go.   145

MADAMOISELLE.
   Demeurez donc.

LADY FANCYFULL.
   Je suis poltrone.

MADAMOISELLE.
   Tant pis pour vous.

LADY FANCYFULL.
   Curiosity's a wicked devil.

MADAMOISELLE.
   C'est une charmante sainte.   150

144. *Je n'en*] *Q3, P; I'n'en Q1–2.*

132–135. *va ... scrupules*] go quickly. Come, madam, hurry. My God,
what scruples!
   140–144. *Belle ... moi*] "A fine thing, delicacy, when it's a question of
amusing oneself. Now, there you're ready, let's go. Well, what is it now?"
"I'm afraid." "I'm not in the least."
   146–148. *Demeurez ... vous.*] "Stay then." "I'm a coward." "So much
the worse for you."
   150. *C'est ... sainte*] It's a charming saint.

LADY FANCYFULL.

It ruined our first parents.

MADAMOISELLE.

Elle a bien diverti leurs enfants.

LADY FANCYFULL.

L'honneur est contre.

MADAMOISELLE.

Le plaisir est pour.

LADY FANCYFULL.

Must I then go?   155

MADAMOISELLE.

Must you go? Must you eat, must you drink, must you sleep, must you live? De nature bid you do one, de nature bid you do toder. *Vous me ferez enrager.*

LADY FANCYFULL.

But when reason corrects nature, Madamoiselle?

MADAMOISELLE.

Elle est donc bien insolente. C'est sa sœur aînée.   160

LADY FANCYFULL.

Do you then prefer your nature to your reason, Madam-oiselle?

MADAMOISELLE.

Oui da.

LADY FANCYFULL.

Pourquoi?

MADAMOISELLE.

Because my nature make me merry, my reason make me 165 mad.

LADY FANCYFULL.

Ah la méchante française.

MADAMOISELLE.

Ah la belle anglaise.   *Forcing her lady off.*

152–154. *Elle . . . pour*] "It has amused their children well." "Honor is against it." "Pleasure is for it."

158. *Vous . . . enrager*] You make me furious.

160. *Elle . . . aînée*] Then she is very insolent. It is her elder sister.

163–164. *Oui da. Pourquoi?*] "Yes indeed." "Why?"

167–168. *Ah . . . anglaise*] "Ah the wicked Frenchwoman." "Ah the beautiful Englishwoman."

ACT II

St. James's Park.
Enter Lady Fancyfull *and* Madamoiselle.

LADY FANCYFULL.

Well, I vow, Madamoiselle, I'm strangely impatient to know
who this confident fellow is.

Enter Heartfree.

Look, there's Heartfree. But sure it can't be him, he's a
professed woman-hater. Yet who knows what my wicked
eyes may have done?   5

MADAMOISELLE.

Il nous approche, madam.

LADY FANCYFULL.

Yes, 'tis he. Now will he be most intolerably cavalier,
though he should be in love with me.

HEARTFREE.

Madam, I'm your humble servant. I perceive you have
more humility and good nature than I thought you had.   10

LADY FANCYFULL.

What you attribute to humility and good nature, sir, may
perhaps be only due to curiosity. I had a mind to know who
'twas had ill manners enough to write that letter.

Throwing him his letter.

HEARTFREE.

Well, and now, I hope, you are satisfied.

LADY FANCYFULL.

I am so, sir. Goodbye to ye.   15

HEARTFREE.

Nay, hold there! Though you have done your business I
han't done mine. By your ladyship's leave, we must have one
moment's prattle together. Have you a mind to be the
prettiest woman about town, or not? How she stares upon
me! What? This passes for an impertinent question with   20
you now, because you think you are so already.

LADY FANCYFULL.

Pray sir, let me ask you a question in my turn. By what right
do you pretend to examine me?

---

6. *Il nous approche*] He is coming toward us.

HEARTFREE.

> By the same right that the strong govern the weak, because
> I have you in my power; for you cannot get so quickly to   25
> your coach but I shall have time enough to make you hear
> everything I have to say to you.

LADY FANCYFULL.

> These are strange liberties you take, Mr. Heartfree.

HEARTFREE.

> They are so, madam, but there's no help for it; for know,
> that I have a design upon you.   30

LADY FANCYFULL.

> Upon me, sir?

HEARTFREE.

> Yes, and one that will turn to your glory and my comfort,
> if you will but be a little wiser than you use to be.

LADY FANCYFULL.

> Very well, sir.

HEARTFREE.

> Let me see. Your vanity, madam, I take to be about some   35
> eight degrees higher than any woman's in the town, let
> t'other be who she will; and my indifference is naturally
> about the same pitch. Now, could you find the way to turn
> this indifference into fire and flames, methinks your vanity
> ought to be satisfied; and this, perhaps, you might bring   40
> about upon pretty reasonable terms.

LADY FANCYFULL.

> And pray at what rate would this indifference be bought off,
> if one should have so depraved an appetite to desire it?

HEARTFREE.

> Why, madam, to drive a Quaker's bargain, and make but
> one word with you, if I do part with it, you must lay me   45
> down—your affectation.

LADY FANCYFULL.

> My affectation, sir!

HEARTFREE.

> Why, I ask you nothing but what you may very well spare.

LADY FANCYFULL.

> You grow rude, sir. Come, Madamoiselle, 'tis high time to
> be gone.   50

---

44. *Quaker's bargain*] a take-it-or-leave-it proposition.

MADAMOISELLE.

Allons, allons, allons!

HEARTFREE *(stopping 'em)*.

Nay, you may as well stand still, for hear me you shall, walk
which way you please.

LADY FANCYFULL.

What mean you, sir?

HEARTFREE.

I mean to tell you that you are the most ungrateful woman 55
upon earth.

LADY FANCYFULL.

Ungrateful! To who?

HEARTFREE.

To nature.

LADY FANCYFULL.

Why, what has nature done for me?

HEARTFREE.

What you have undone by art. It made you handsome, it 60
gave you beauty to a miracle, a shape without a fault, wit
enough to make 'em relish, and so turned you loose to your
own discretion, which has made such work with you that
you are become the pity of our sex and the jest of your own.
There is not a feature in your face but you have found the 65
way to teach it some affected convulsion; your feet, your
hands, your very fingers' ends are directed never to move
without some ridiculous air or other, and your language is
a suitable trumpet to draw people's eyes upon the raree-
show. 70

MADAMOISELLE *(aside)*.

Est ce qu'on fait l'amour en Angleterre comme ça?

LADY FANCYFULL *(aside)*.

Now could I cry for madness, but that I know he'd laugh at
me for it.

HEARTFREE.

Now do you hate me for telling you the truth, but that's
because you don't believe it is so; for were you once 75

52. S.D. *'em*] Q1–3; *them* P.

---

51. *Allons*] come.
69–70. *raree-show*] a peep-show carried in a box.
71. *Est . . . ça?*] Is this the way one makes love in England?

convinced of that, you'd reform for your own sake. But 'tis as
hard to persuade a woman to quit anything that makes her
ridiculous as 'tis to prevail with a poet to see a fault in his
own play.

LADY FANCYFULL.

Every circumstance of nice breeding must needs appear   80
ridiculous to one who has so natural an antipathy to good
manners.

HEARTFREE.

But suppose I could find the means to convince you that the
whole world is of my opinion, and that those who flatter and
commend you do it to no other intent but to make you   85
persevere in your folly that they may continue in their
mirth.

LADY FANCYFULL.

Sir, though you and all that world you talk of should be so
impertinently officious as to think to persuade me I don't
know how to behave myself, I should still have charity   90
enough for my own understanding to believe myself in the
right, and all you in the wrong.

MADAMOISELLE.

Le voilà mort.   *Exeunt* Lady Fancyfull *and* Madamoiselle.

HEARTFREE *(gazing after her)*.

There her single clapper has published the sense of the
whole sex. Well, this once I have endeavored to wash the   95
blackamoor white, but henceforward I'll sooner undertake
to teach sincerity to a courtier, generosity to an usurer,
honesty to a lawyer, nay, humility to a divine, than discretion to a woman I see has once set her heart upon
playing the fool.   100

Enter Constant.

'Morrow, Constant.

CONSTANT.

Good morrow, Jack. What are you doing here this morning?

HEARTFREE.

Doing! Guess if thou canst. Why, I have been endeavoring
to persuade my Lady Fancyfull that she's the foolishest
woman about town.   105

---

93 *Le ... mort*] That killed him.   94. *clapper*] tongue.

CONSTANT.

A pretty endeavor, truly.

HEARTFREE.

I have told her in as plain English as I could speak, both
what the town says of her and what I think of her. In short,
I have used her as an absolute king would do Magna Charta.

CONSTANT.

And how does she take it?   110

HEARTFREE.

As children do pills: bite 'em, but can't swallow 'em.

CONSTANT.

But, prithee, what has put it in your head, of all mankind,
to turn reformer?

HEARTFREE.

Why, one thing was, the morning hung upon my hands, I
did not know what to do with myself. And another was, that 115
as little as I care for women, I could not see with patience
one that heaven had taken such wondrous pains about be
so very industrious to make herself the jack-pudding of the
creation.

CONSTANT.

Well, now could I almost wish to see my cruel mistress 120
make the selfsame use of what heaven has done for her, that
so I might be cured of a disease that makes me so very
uneasy; for love, love is the devil, Heartfree.

HEARTFREE.

And why do you let the devil govern you?

CONSTANT.

Because I have more flesh and blood than grace and self- 125
denial. My dear, dear mistress—'sdeath, that so genteel a
woman should be a saint when religion's out of fashion!

HEARTFREE.

Nay, she's much in the wrong truly; but who knows how
far time and good example may prevail?

CONSTANT.

O, they have played their parts in vain already. 'Tis now 130
two years since that damned fellow her husband invited me
to his wedding, and there was the first time I saw that

112. in] *Q1–2*; into *Q3, P.*

charming woman, whom I have loved ever since more than
e'er a martyr did his soul. But she's cold, my friend, still
cold as the northern star.   135

HEARTFREE.

So are all women by nature, which makes 'em so willing to be
warmed.

CONSTANT.

O, don't profane the sex; prithee think 'em all angels for her
sake, for she's virtuous even to a fault.

HEARTFREE.

A lover's head is a good accountable thing truly: he adores 140
his mistress for being virtuous and yet is very angry with her
because she won't be lewd.

CONSTANT.

Well, the only relief I expect in my misery is to see thee
some day or other as deeply engaged as myself, which will
force me to be merry in the midst of all my misfortunes.   145

HEARTFREE.

That day will never come, be assured, Ned. Not but that I
can pass a night with a woman, and for the time, perhaps,
make myself as good sport as you can do. Nay, I can court
a woman too, call her nymph, angel, goddess, what you
please; but here's the difference 'twixt you and I: I persuade 150
a woman she's an angel; she persuades you she's one. Prithee
let me tell you how I avoid falling in love; that which serves
me for prevention may chance to serve you for a cure.

CONSTANT.

Well, use the ladies moderately then, and I'll hear you.

HEARTFREE.

That using 'em moderately undoes us all; but I'll use 'em 155
justly, and that you ought to be satisfied with. I always
consider a woman, not as the tailor, the shoemaker, the
tire-woman, the seamstress, and (which is more than all
that) the poet makes her, but I consider her as pure nature
has contrived her, and that more strictly than I should have 160
done our old Grandmother Eve, had I seen her naked in the
Garden, for I consider her turned inside out. Her heart well

151. she] *Q1–2*; and she *Q3, P*.   158. and (which] *Q3, P*; (and which
                                                     Q1–2.

examined, I find there pride, vanity, covetousness, indis-
cretion, but above all things malice—plots eternally aforging
to destroy one another's reputations and as honestly to 165
charge the levity of men's tongues with the scandal, hourly
debates how to make poor gentlemen in love with 'em with
no other intent but to use 'em like dogs when they have
done, a constant desire of doing more mischief, and an
everlasting war waged against truth and good nature. 170

CONSTANT.

Very well, sir, an admirable composition truly.

HEARTFREE.

Then for her outside, I consider it merely as an outside; she
has a thin tiffany covering over just such stuff as you and I
are made on. As for her motion, her mein, her airs, and all
those tricks, I know they affect you mightily. If you should 175
see your mistress at a coronation, dragging her peacock's
train, with all her state and insolence about her, 'twould
strike you with all the awful thoughts that heaven itself
could pretend to from you; whereas I turn the whole matter
into a jest, and suppose her strutting in the self-same stately 180
manner with nothing on but her stays and her under scanty
quilted petticoat.

CONSTANT.

Hold thy profane tongue, for I'll hear no more.

HEARTFREE.

What, you'll love on, then?

CONSTANT.

Yes, to eternity. 185

HEARTFREE.

Yet you have no hopes at all?

CONSTANT.

None.

HEARTFREE.

Nay, the resolution may be discreet enough. Perhaps you
have found out some new philosophy, that love's like virtue,
its own reward; so you and your mistress will be as well con- 190
tent at a distance as others that have less learning are in
coming together.

CONSTANT.

No, but if she should prove kind at last, my dear Heartfree!
Embracing him.

HEARTFREE.

Nay, prithee don't take me for your mistress, for lovers are
very troublesome.   195

CONSTANT.

Well, who knows what time may do?

HEARTFREE.

And just now he was sure time could do nothing.

CONSTANT.

Yet not one kind glance in two years is somewhat strange.

HEARTFREE.

Not strange at all. She don't like you, that's all the business.

CONSTANT.

Prithee don't distract me.   200

HEARTFREE.

Nay, you are a good handsome young fellow; she might use
you better. Come, will you go see her? Perhaps she may
have changed her mind; there's some hopes as long as she's
a woman.

CONSTANT.

O, 'tis in vain to visit her. Sometimes to get a sight of her I   205
visit that beast her husband, but she certainly finds some
pretense to quit the room as soon as I enter.

HEARTFREE.

It's much she don't tell him you have made love to her, too,
for that's another good-natured thing usual amongst women,
in which they have several ends. Sometimes 'tis to recom-   210
mend their virtue, that they may be lewd with the greater
security. Sometimes 'tis to make their husbands fight in
hopes they may be killed, when their affairs require it should
be so. But most commonly 'tis to engage two men in a
quarrel that they may have the credit of being fought for;   215
and if the lover's killed in the business, they cry, "Poor
fellow! he had ill luck"—and so they go to cards.

CONSTANT.

Thy injuries to women are not to be forgiven. Look to't if
ever thou dost fall into their hands.

HEARTFREE.

They can't use me worse than they do you, that speak well   220
of 'em. Oho! Here comes the knight.

Enter Sir John Brute.

Your humble servant, Sir John.

SIR JOHN.

Servant, sir.

HEARTFREE.

How does all your family?

SIR JOHN.

Pox o' my family.   225

CONSTANT.

How does your lady? I han't seen her abroad a good while.

SIR JOHN.

Do? I don't know how she does, not I. She was well enough
yesterday; I han't been at home tonight.

CONSTANT.

What, were you out of town?

SIR JOHN.

Out of town? No, I was drinking.   230

CONSTANT.

You are a true Englishman, don't know your own happiness.
If I were married to such a woman I would not be from her
a night for all the wine in France.

SIR JOHN.

Not from her? Oons, what a time should a man have of
that?   235

HEARTFREE.

Why, there's no division, I hope?

SIR JOHN.

No, but there's a conjunction, and that's worse; a pox o' the
parson. Why the plague don't you two marry? I fancy I
look like the devil to you.

HEARTFREE.

Why, you don't think you have horns, do you?   240

SIR JOHN.

No, I believe my wife's religion will keep her honest.

HEARTFREE.

And what will make her keep her religion?

SIR JOHN.

Persecution; and therefore she shall have it.

---

237. *conjunction*] Astrologically, a conjunction of two planets was usually
malign.

HEARTFREE.

Have a care, knight; women are tender things.

SIR JOHN.

And yet, methinks, 'tis a hard matter to break their hearts. 245

CONSTANT.

Fie, fie, you have one of the best wives in the world, and yet
you seem the most uneasy husband.

SIR JOHN.

Best wives! The woman's well enough, she has no vice that
I know of, but she's a wife and— Damn a wife! If I were
married to a hogshead of claret, matrimony would make me 250
hate it.

HEARTFREE.

Why did you marry then? You were old enough to know
your own mind.

SIR JOHN.

Why did I marry? I married because I had a mind to lie
with her, and she would not let me. 255

HEARTFREE.

Why did not you ravish her?

SIR JOHN.

Yes, and so have hedged myself into forty quarrels with her
relations, besides buying my pardon. But more than all that,
you must know I was afraid of being damned in those days,
for I kept sneaking cowardly company, fellows that went to 260
church, said grace to their meat, and had not the least
tincture of quality about 'em.

HEARTFREE.

But I think you are got into a better gang now.

SIR JOHN.

Zounds, sir, my Lord Rake and I are hand in glove; I
believe we may get our bones broke together tonight. Have 265
you a mind to share a frolic?

CONSTANT.

Not I, truly; my talent lies to softer exercises.

SIR JOHN.

What, a down bed and a strumpet? A pox of venery, I say.

256. not you] *Q1–2*; you not *Q3,*
P.

Will you come and drink with me this afternoon?

CONSTANT.

    I can't drink today, but we'll come and sit an hour with you 270
if you will.

SIR JOHN.

    Pugh, pox, sit an hour! Why can't you drink?

CONSTANT.

    Because I'm to see my mistress.

SIR JOHN.

    Who's that?

CONSTANT.

    Why, do you use to tell?   275

SIR JOHN.

    Yes.

CONSTANT.

    So won't I.

SIR JOHN.

    Why?

CONSTANT.

    Because 'tis a secret.

SIR JOHN.

    Would my wife knew it, 'twould be no secret long.   280

CONSTANT.

    Why, do you think she can't keep a secret?

SIR JOHN.

    No more than she can keep Lent.

HEARTFREE.

    Prithee, tell it her to try, Constant.

SIR JOHN.

    No, prithee don't, that I mayn't be plagued with it.

CONSTANT.

    I'll hold you a guinea you don't make her tell it you.   285

SIR JOHN.

    I'll hold you a guinea I do.

CONSTANT.

    Which way?

SIR JOHN.

    Why, I'll beg her not to tell it me.

HEARTFREE.

    Nay, if anything does it, that will.

CONSTANT.

But do you think, sir—?   290

SIR JOHN.

Oons, sir, I think a woman and a secret are the two imper-
tinentest themes in the universe. Therefore pray let's hear
no more of my wife nor your mistress. Damn 'em both with
all my heart, and everything else that daggles a petticoat,
except four generous whores, with Betty Sands at the head 295
of 'em, who were drunk with my Lord Rake and I ten times
in a fortnight.   *Exit* Sir John.

CONSTANT.

Here's a dainty fellow for you. And the veriest coward, too.
But his usage of his wife makes me ready to stab the villain.

HEARTFREE.

Lovers are short-sighted; all their senses run into that of 300
feeling. This proceeding of his is the only thing on earth can
make your fortune. If anything can prevail with her to
accept of a gallant 'tis his ill usage of her, for women will do
more for revenge than they'll do for the gospel. Prithee take
heart, I have great hopes for you, and since I can't bring you 305
quite off of her, I'll endeavor to bring you quite on; for a
whining lover is damnedest companion upon earth.

CONSTANT.

My dear friend, flatter me a little more with these hopes;
for whilst they prevail I have heaven within me and could
melt with joy.   310

HEARTFREE.

Pray, no melting yet; let things go farther first. This afternoon perhaps we shall make some advance. In the mean-
while, let's go dine at Locket's, and let hope get you a
stomach.   *Exeunt.*

[II.ii]   *Lady Fancyfull's house.*
                 Enter Lady Fancyfull *and* Madamoiselle.

LADY FANCYFULL.

Did you ever see anything so importune, Madamoiselle?

---

294. *daggles*] trails through the mire.
313. *Locket's*] the most fashionable tavern.

MADAMOISELLE.

Inteed, Matam, to say de trute, he want leetel good breeding.

LADY FANCYFULL.

Good breeding? He wants to be caned, Madamoiselle. An insolent fellow! And yet let me expose my weakness, 'tis the only man on earth I could resolve to dispense my favors on, 5 were he but a fine gentleman. Well, did men but know how deep an impression a fine gentleman makes in a lady's heart, they would reduce all their studies to that of good breeding alone.

Enter Cornet.

CORNET.

Madam, here's Mr. Treble. He has brought home the verses 10 your ladyship made and gave him to set.

LADY FANCYFULL.

O let him come in, by all means. Now, Madamoiselle, I am going to be unspeakably happy.

Enter Treble.

So, Mr. Treble, you have set my little dialogue?

TREBLE.

Yes, madam, and I hope your ladyship will be pleased with 15 it.

LADY FANCYFULL.

O, no doubt on't, for really, Mr. Treble, you set all things to a wonder. But your music is in particular heavenly when you have my words to clothe in't.

TREBLE.

Your words themselves, madam, have so much music in 'em 20 they inspire me.

LADY FANCYFULL.

Nay, now you make me blush, Mr. Treble. But pray let's hear what you have done.

TREBLE.

You shall, madam.

A Song to be Sung between a Man and a Woman

MAN.   Ah lovely nymph, the world's on fire;   25
               Veil, veil those cruel eyes.

WOMAN.   The world may then in flames expire,
               And boast that so it dies.

2. want] *Q1*; wanted *Q2–3, P.*

MAN.   But when all mortals are destroyed,
                Who then shall sing your praise?   30
WOMAN.   Those who are fit to be employed:
                The gods shall altars raise.

TREBLE.

How does your ladyship like it, madam?

LADY FANCYFULL.

Rapture, rapture, Mr. Treble, I'm all rapture. O wit and
art, what power you have when joined! I must needs tell   35
you the birth of this little dialogue, Mr. Treble. Its father
was a dream and its mother was the moon. I dreamt that by
an unanimous vote I was chosen queen of that pale world.
And that the first time I appeared upon my throne—all my
subjects fell in love with me. Just then I waked, and seeing 40
pen, ink, and paper lie idle upon the table, I slid into my
morning gown and writ this impromptu.

TREBLE.

So I guess the dialogue, madam, is supposed to be between your majesty and your first minister of state.

LADY FANCYFULL.

Just. He as minister advises me to trouble my head about 45
the welfare of my subjects, which I as sovereign find a very
impertinent proposal. But is the town so dull, Mr. Treble, it
affords us never another new song?

TREBLE.

Madam, I have one in my pocket, came out but yesterday,
if your ladyship pleases to let Mrs. Pipe sing it.   50

LADY FANCYFULL.

By all means. Here, Pipe, make what music you can of this
song here.

SONG

[PIPE.]   Not an angel dwells above
                Half so fair as her I love;
                    Heaven knows how she'll receive me.   55
                If she smiles, I'm blest indeed,
                If she frowns, I'm quickly freed;
                    Heaven knows, she ne'er can grieve me.

35. you have] *Q1–2*; have you *Q3,*   50. Mrs. Pipe] *Q1*; Mr. Pipe *Q2–3,*
P.   *P.*

II

None can love her more than I,
Yet she ne'er shall make me die   60
   If my flame can never warm her.
Lasting beauty I'll adore;
I shall never love her more,
   Cruelty will so deform her.

LADY FANCYFULL.
Very well. This is Heartfree's poetry without question.   65
TREBLE.
Won't your ladyship please to sing yourself this morning?
LADY FANCYFULL.
O Lord, Mr. Treble, my cold is still so barbarous to refuse
me that pleasure, he, he, hem.
TREBLE.
I'm very sorry for it, madam; methinks all mankind should
turn physicians for the cure on't.   70
LADY FANCYFULL.
Why truly to give mankind their due, there's few that know
me but have offered their remedy.
TREBLE.
They have reason, madam, for I know nobody sings so near
a cherubin as your ladyship.
LADY FANCYFULL.
What I do I owe chiefly to your skill and care, Mr. Treble.   75
People do flatter me indeed, that I have a voice and a *je ne
sais quoi* in the conduct of it that will make music of any-
thing. And truly I begin to believe so, since what happened
t'other night: would you think it, Mr. Treble, walking
pretty late in the Park (for I often walk late in the Park, Mr.   80
Treble), a whim took me to sing Chevy-Chase, and would
you believe it? Next morning I had three copies of verses and
six billet-doux at my levee upon it.
TREBLE.
And without all dispute you deserved as many more, madam.

---

74. *cherubin*] cherub. Cherubin was a common (if formally incorrect)
singular form.
76–77. *je ne sais quoi*] I know not what.

Are there any further commands for your ladyship's humble   85
servant?

LADY FANCYFULL.

Nothing more at this time, Mr. Treble. But I shall expect
you here every morning for this month, to sing my little
matter there to me. I'll reward you for your pains.

TREBLE.

O Lord, madam—   90

LADY FANCYFULL.

Good morrow, sweet Mr. Treble.

TREBLE.

Your ladyship's most obedient servant.   *Exit* Treble.

Enter Servant.

SERVANT.

Will your ladyship please to dine yet?

LADY FANCYFULL.

Yes, let 'em serve.   *Exit* Servant.
Sure this Heartfree has bewitched me, Madamoiselle. You   95
can't imagine how oddly he mixed himself in my thoughts
during my rapture e'en now. I vow 'tis a thousand pities he
is not more polished. Don't you think so?

MADAMOISELLE.

Matam, I tink it so great pity, dat if I was in your ladyship
place, I take him home in my house, I lock him up in my   100
closet, and I never let him go till I teach him everyting dat
fine laty expect from fine gentleman.

LADY FANCYFULL.

Why truly I believe I should soon subdue his brutality; for
without doubt he has a strange penchant to grow fond of me
in spite of his aversion to the sex, else he would ne'er have   105
taken so much pains about me. Lord, how proud would
some poor creatures be of such a conquest! But I, alas, I
don't know how to receive as a favor what I take to be so
infinitely my due. But what shall I do to new-mold him,
Madamoiselle? For till then he's my utter aversion.   110

MADAMOISELLE.

Matam, you must laugh at him in all de place dat you meet
him, and turn into de ridicule all he say and all he do.

LADY FANCYFULL.

Why truly satire has been ever of wondrous use to reform ill
manners. Besides 'tis my particular talent to ridicule folks.
I can be severe, strangely severe, when I will, Madamoiselle. 115
Give me the pen and ink—I find myself whimsical—I'll
write to him. (*Sitting down to write.*) Or I'll let it alone
and be severe upon him that way. (*Rising up again.*) Yet
active severity is better than passive. (*Sitting down.*) 'Tis
as good let alone too, for every lash I give him perhaps he'll 120
take for a favor. (*Rising.*) Yet 'tis a thousand pities so
much satire should be lost. (*Sitting.*) But if it should have
a wrong effect upon him 'twould distract me. (*Rising.*)
Well I must write though after all. (*Sitting.*) Or I'll let it
alone, which is the same thing. (*Rising.*)   125

MADAMOISELLE.

La voilà determinée.   *Exeunt.*

113. been ever] *Q1–2*; ever been   120. let] *Q1–2*; let it *Q3, P.*
Q3, P.

---

126. *La voilà determinée*] She's determined.

ACT III

[*Sir John Brute's House*].

Scene opens. Sir John, Lady Brute, *and* Bellinda *rising from the table*.

SIR JOHN (*to a servant*).

> Here, take away the things, I expect company. But first
> bring me a pipe; I'll smoke.

LADY BRUTE.

> Lord, Sir John, I wonder you won't leave that nasty custom.

SIR JOHN.

> Prithee don't be impertinent.

BELLINDA (*to* Lady Brute).

> I wonder who those are he expects this afternoon.   5

LADY BRUTE.

> I'd give the world to know. Perhaps 'tis Constant; he comes
> here sometimes. If it does prove him, I'm resolved I'll share
> the visit.

BELLINDA.

> We'll send for our work and sit here.

LADY BRUTE.

> He'll choke us with his tobacco.   10

BELLINDA.

> Nothing will choke us when we are doing what we have a
> mind to. Lovewell!

Enter Lovewell.

LOVEWELL.

> Madam?

LADY BRUTE.

> Here, bring my cousin's work and mine hither.

> > *Exit* Lovewell *and re-enters with their work*.

SIR JOHN.

> Why, pox, can't you work somewhere else?   15

LADY BRUTE.

> We shall be careful not to disturb you, sir.

BELLINDA.

> Your pipe would make you too thoughtful, uncle, if you

17. would] *Q1*; will *Q2–3, P.*

12.] Q1 has a very long space before "Lovewell." It is possible that a
speech prefix was dropped and that Lady Brute called her servant.

were left alone. Our prittle-prattle will cure your spleen.

SIR JOHN.

Will it so, Mrs. Pert? Now I believe it will so increase it I
shall take my own house for a paper mill. *Sitting and smoking.* 20

LADY BRUTE (*to* Bellinda *aside*).

Don't let's mind him; let him say what he will.

SIR JOHN.

A woman's tongue a cure for the spleen! Oons! (*Aside.*)
If a man had got the headache, they'd be for applying the
same remedy.

LADY BRUTE.

You have done a great deal, Bellinda, since yesterday. 25

BELLINDA.

Yes, I have worked very hard; how do you like it?

LADY BRUTE.

O, 'tis the prettiest fringe in the world. Well, cousin, you
have the happiest fancy. Prithee advise me about altering
my crimson petticoat.

SIR JOHN.

A pox o' your petticoat! Here's such a prating a man can't 30
digest his own thoughts for you.

LADY BRUTE (*aside.*)

Don't answer him.—Well, what do you advise me?

BELLINDA.

Why, really, I would not alter it at all. Methinks 'tis very
pretty as it is.

LADY BRUTE.

Aye, that's true. But you know one grows weary of the 35
prettiest things in the world when one has had 'em long.

SIR JOHN.

Yes, I have taught her that.

BELLINDA.

Shall we provoke him a little?

LADY BRUTE.

With all my heart.—Bellinda, don't you long to be married?

BELLINDA.

Why, there are some things in't I could like well enough. 40

---

20. *paper mill*] Cf. Etherege, *Love in a Tub:* "She's made more noise than
half a dozen paper mills."

LADY BRUTE.

What do you think you should dislike?

BELLINDA.

My husband, a hundred to one else.

LADY BRUTE.

O ye wicked wretch, sure you don't speak as you think.

BELLINDA.

Yes I do; especially if he smoked tobacco.

He looks earnestly at 'em.

LADY BRUTE.

Why, that many times takes off worse smells.   45

BELLINDA.

Then he must smell very ill indeed.

LADY BRUTE.

So some men will, to keep their wives from coming near 'em.

BELLINDA.

Then those wives should cuckold 'em at a distance.

He rises in a fury, throws his pipe at 'em and drives 'em out. As they run off,
Constant *and* Heartfree *enter.* Lady Brute *runs against* Constant.

SIR JOHN.

Oons, get you gone upstairs, you confederating strumpets
you, or I'll cuckold you with a vengeance.   50

LADY BRUTE.

O Lord, he'll beat us, he'll beat us. Dear, dear Mr. Constant, save us.   *Exeunt* [Lady Brute *and* Bellinda].

SIR JOHN.

I'll cuckold you, with a pox.

CONSTANT.

Heavens, Sir John, what's the matter?

SIR JOHN.

Sure if woman had been ready created, the devil, instead of   55
being kicked down into hell, had been married.

HEARTFREE.

Why, what new plague have you found now?

SIR JOHN.

Why, these two gentlewomen did but hear me say I expected
you here this afternoon, upon which they presently resolved

55. woman] *Q1-2*; women *Q3, P.*

to take up the room, o' purpose to plague me and my friends.

CONSTANT.

Was that all? Why, we should have been glad of their company.

SIR JOHN.

Then I should have been weary of yours. For I can't relish both together. They found fault with my smoking tobacco 65 too, and said men stunk. But I have a good mind—to say something.

CONSTANT.

No, nothing against the ladies, pray.

SIR JOHN.

Split the ladies. Come, will you sit down? Give us some wine, fellow. You won't smoke?   70

CONSTANT.

No, nor drink neither, at this time; I must ask your pardon.

SIR JOHN.

What, this mistress of yours runs in your head; I'll warrant it's some such squeamish minx as my wife, that's grown so dainty of late she finds fault even with a dirty shirt.

HEARTFREE.

That a woman may do, and not be very dainty neither.   75

SIR JOHN.

Pox o' the women, let's drink. Come, you shall take one glass, though I send for a box of lozenges to sweeten your mouth after it.

CONSTANT.

Nay, if one glass will satisfy you I'll drink it without putting you to that expense.   80

SIR JOHN.

Why that's honest. Fill some wine, sirrah! So, here's to you, gentlemen—a wife's the devil. To your being both married.

They drink.

HEARTFREE.

O' your most humble servant, sir.

SIR JOHN.

Well? How do you like my wine?

CONSTANT.

'Tis very good indeed.   85

HEARTFREE.

'Tis admirable.

SIR JOHN.

Then give us t'other glass.

CONSTANT.

No, pray excuse us now. We'll come another time, and then we won't spare it.

SIR JOHN.

This one glass and no more. Come, it shall be your mis- 90
tresses' health; and that's a great compliment from me, I assure you.

CONSTANT.

And 'tis a very obliging one to me. So give us the glasses.

SIR JOHN.

So. Let her live.

HEARTFREE.

And be kind.   Sir John *coughs in the glass.* 95

CONSTANT.

What's the matter? Does't go the wrong way?

SIR JOHN.

If I had love enough to be jealous, I should take this for an ill omen. For I never drank my wife's health in my life but I puked in the glass.

CONSTANT.

Oh, she's too virtuous to make a reasonable man jealous. 100

SIR JOHN.

Pox of her virtue. If I could but catch her adulterating I might be divorced from her by law.

HEARTFREE.

And so pay her a yearly pension to be a distinguished cuckold.

Enter Servant.

[SERVANT].

Sir, there's my Lord Rake, Colonel Bully, and some other 105
gentlemen at the Blue Posts desire your company.   [*Exit.*]

96. Does't] *Q1*; Does it *Q2–3, P.*

---

103. *yearly pension*] See note to I.i.53–54.
106. *Blue Posts*] an inn in the Haymarket.

SIR JOHN.

Cod's so, we are to consult about playing the devil tonight.

HEARTFREE.

Well, we won't hinder business.

SIR JOHN.

Methinks I don't know how to leave you, though. But for
once I must make bold. Or look you, maybe the conference 110
mayn't last long, so if you'll wait here half an hour or an
hour, if I don't come then—why then—I won't come at all.

HEARTFREE (*to* Constant, *aside*).

A good, modest proposition, truly.

CONSTANT.

But let's accept on't, however. Who knows what may
happen.   115

HEARTFREE.

Well, sir, to show you how fond we are of your company
we'll expect your return as long as we can.

SIR JOHN.

Nay, maybe I mayn't stay at all; but business you know
must be done. So, your servant—or, hark you: if you have
a mind to take a frisk with us, I have an interest with my 120
lord, I can easily introduce you.

CONSTANT.

We are much beholding to you, but for my part I'm engaged
another way.

SIR JOHN.

What? To your mistress, I'll warrant. Prithee leave your
nasty punk to entertain herself with her own lewd thoughts 125
and make one with us tonight.

CONSTANT.

Sir, 'tis business that is to employ me.

HEARTFREE.

And me; and business must be done, you know.

SIR JOHN.

Aye, women's business, though the world were consumed
for't.   *Exit* Sir John. 130

122. beholding] *Q1–3*; beholden *P*.

---

117. *expect*] await.

CONSTANT.

Farewell, beast. And now, my dear friend, would my
mistress be but as complaisant as some men's wives, who
think it a piece of good breeding to receive the visits of their
husband's friends in his absence.

HEARTFREE.

Why, for your sake I could forgive her, though she should 135
be so complaisant to receive something else in his absence.
But what way shall we invent to see her?

CONSTANT.

O ne'er hope it. Invention will prove as vain as wishes.

Enter Lady Brute *and* Bellinda.

HEARTFREE.

What do you think now, friend?

CONSTANT.

I think I shall swoon. 140

HEARTFREE.

I'll speak first then, whilst you fetch breath.

LADY BRUTE.

We think ourselves obliged, gentlemen, to come and return
you thanks for your knight-errantry. We were just upon
being devoured by the fiery dragon.

BELLINDA.

Did not his fumes almost knock you down, gentlemen? 145

HEARTFREE.

Truly, ladies, we did undergo some hardships, and should
have done more, if some greater heroes than ourselves hard
by had not diverted him.

CONSTANT.

Though I am glad of the service you are pleased to say we
have done you, yet I'm sorry we could do it no other way 150
than by making ourselves privy to what you would perhaps
have kept a secret.

LADY BRUTE.

For Sir John's part, I suppose he designed it no secret, since
he made so much noise. And for myself, truly I am not much
concerned, since 'tis fallen only into this gentleman's hands 155
and yours, who I have many reasons to believe will neither
interpret nor report anything to my disadvantage.

150. no] *Q1–3*; in no *P.*

CONSTANT.

Your good opinion, madam, was what I feared I never could
have merited.

LADY BRUTE.

Your fears were vain then, sir, for I am just to everybody. 160

HEARTFREE.

Prithee, Constant, what is't you do to get the ladies' good
opinions, for I'm a novice at it?

BELLINDA.

Sir, will you give me leave to instruct you?

HEARTFREE.

Yes, that I will with all my soul, madam.

BELLINDA.

Why then you must never be slovenly, never be out of 165
humor, fare well and cry roast-meat, smoke tobacco, nor
drink but when you are a-dry.

HEARTFREE.

That's hard.

CONSTANT.

Nay, if you take his bottle from him you break his heart,
madam.   170

BELLINDA.

Why, is it possible the gentleman can love drinking?

HEARTFREE.

Only by way of antidote.

BELLINDA.

Against what, pray?

HEARTFREE.

Against love, madam.

LADY BRUTE.

Are you afraid of being in love, sir?   175

HEARTFREE.

I should, if there were any danger of it.

LADY BRUTE.

Pray why so?

HEARTFREE.

Because I always had an aversion to being used like a dog.

---

166. *cry roast-meat*] brag about good fortune.

BELLINDA.

Why truly, men in love are seldom used better.

LADY BRUTE.

But was you never in love, sir?

HEARTFREE.

No, I thank heaven, madam.

BELLINDA.

Pray, where got you your leaning then?

HEARTFREE.

From other people's expense.

BELLINDA.

That's being a sponger, sir, which is scarce honest; if you'd
buy some experience with your own money, as 'twould be 185
fairlier got, so 'twould stick longer by you.

Enter Footman.

FOOTMAN.

Madam, here's my Lady Fancyfull to wait upon your
ladyship.

LADY BRUTE.

Shield me, kind heaven, what an inundation of impertinence is here coming upon us!   190

Enter Lady Fancyfull, *who runs first to* Lady Brute, *then to* Bellinda,
kissing 'em.

LADY FANCYFULL.

My dear Lady Brute and sweet Bellinda, methinks 'tis an age
since I saw you.

LADY BRUTE.

Yet 'tis but three days; sure you have passed your time very
ill, it seems so long to you.

LADY FANCYFULL.

Why really, to confess the truth to you, I am so everlastingly 195
fatigued with the addresses of unfortunate gentlemen, that
were it not for the extravagancy of the example I should
e'en tear out these wicked eyes with my own fingers, to make
both myself and mankind easy. What think you on't, Mr.
Heartfree, for I take you to be my faithful adviser?   200

HEARTFREE.

Why truly, madam—I think—every project that is for the
good of mankind ought to be encouraged.

LADY FANCYFULL.

Then I have your consent, sir.

HEARTFREE.

To do whatever you please, madam.

LADY FANCYFULL.

You had a much more limited complaisance this morning, 205
sir. Would you believe it, ladies? The gentleman has been
so exceeding generous to tell me of above fifty faults in less
time than it was well possible for me to commit two of 'em.

CONSTANT.

Why truly, madam, my friend there is apt to be something
familiar with the ladies.   210

LADY FANCYFULL.

He is indeed, sir, but he's wondrous charitable with it; he
has had the goodness to design a reformation, even down to
my fingers' ends. 'Twas thus, I think, sir, you would have
had 'em stand. (*Opening her fingers in an awkward manner.*)
My eyes too he did not like; how was't you would have 215
directed 'em? Thus, I think. (*Staring at him.*)   Then there
was something amiss in my gait, too; I don't know well how
'twas, but as I take it he would have had me walk like him.
Pray, sir, do me the favor to take a turn or two about the
room, that the company may see you. He's sullen, ladies, 220
and won't. But, to make short and give you as true an idea
as I can of the matter, I think 'twas much about this figure
in general, he would have molded me to.

*She walks awkwardly about, staring and looking ungainly, then changes on a
sudden to the extremity of her usual affectation.*

But I was an obstinate woman and could not resolve to make
myself mistress of his heart by growing as awkward as his 225
fancy.   *Here* Constant *and* Lady Brute *talk together apart.*

HEARTFREE.

Just thus women do when they think we are in love with 'em,
or when they are so with us.

LADY FANCYFULL.

'Twould however, be less vanity for me to conclude the
former than you the latter, sir.   230

213. you would] *Q1–2*; you'ld *Q3,*
P.

HEARTFREE.

Madam, all I shall presume to conclude is, that if I were in love, you'd find the means to make me soon weary on't.

LADY FANCYFULL.

Not by overfondness, upon my word, sir. But pray let's stop here, for you are so much governed by instinct I know you'll grow brutish at last. 235

BELLINDA (*aside.*)

Now am I sure she's fond of him; I'll try to make her jealous. —Well, for my part, I should be glad to find somebody would be so free with me, that I might know my faults and mend 'em.

LADY FANCYFULL.

Then pray let me recommend this gentleman to you; I have 240 known him some time and will be surety for him, that upon a very limited encouragement on your side you shall find an extended impudence on his.

HEARTFREE.

I thank you, madam, for your recommendation. But, hating idleness, I'm unwilling to enter into a place where I believe 245 there would be nothing to do. I was fond of serving your ladyship because I knew you'd find me constant employment.

LADY FANCYFULL.

I told you he'd be rude, Bellinda.

BELLINDA.

O, a little bluntness is a sign of honesty, which makes me 250 always ready to pardon it. So, sir, if you have no other exceptions to my service but the fear of being idle in't, you may venture to 'list yourself; I shall find you work, I warrant you.

HEARTFREE.

Upon those terms I engage, madam, and this (with your 255 leave) I take for earnest. *Offering to kiss her hand.*

BELLINDA.

Hold there, sir, I'm none of your earnest-givers. But if I'm well served I give good wages and pay punctually.

Heartfree *and* Bellinda *seem to continue talking familiarly.*

236. am I] *Q1*; I am *Q2–3*; I'm *P.*

LADY FANCYFULL (*aside*).

 I don't like this jesting between 'em. Methinks the fool
begins to look as if he were in earnest—but then he must be 260
a fool indeed. Lard, what a difference there is between me
and her. (*Looking at* Bellinda *scornfully*.) How I should
despise such a thing if I were a man. What a nose she has!
what a chin! what a neck! Then her eyes—and the worst
kissing lips in the universe. No, no, he can never like her, 265
that's positive. Yet I can't suffer 'em together any longer.—
Mr. Heartfree, do you know that you and I must have no
quarrel for all this? I can't forbear being a little severe now
and then; but women, you know, may be allowed anything.

HEARTFREE.

 Up to a certain age, madam.   270

LADY FANCYFULL.

 Which I am not yet past, I hope.

HEARTFREE (*aside*).

 Nor never will, I dare swear.

LADY FANCYFULL (*to* Lady Brute).

 Come, madam, will your ladyship be witness to our recon-
ciliation?

LADY BRUTE.

 You agree then at last?   275

HEARTFREE (*slightingly*).

 We forgive.

LADY FANCYFULL (*aside*).

 That was a cold, ill-natured reply.

LADY BRUTE.

 Then there's no challenges sent between you?

HEARTFREE.

 Not from me, I promise. (*Aside to* Constant.) But that's
more than I'll do for her, for I know she can as well be 280
damned as forbear writing to me.

CONSTANT.

 That I believe. But I think we had best be going lest she
should suspect something and be malicious.

HEARTFREE.

 With all my heart.

CONSTANT.

 Ladies, we are your humble servants. I see Sir John is quite 285 engaged, 'twould be in vain to expect him. Come, Heartfree.

Exit.

HEARTFREE.

Ladies, your servant. (*To* Bellinda.) I hope, madam, you won't forget our bargain; I'm to say what I please to you.

BELLINDA.

Liberty of speech entire, sir. *Exit* Heartfree.

LADY FANCYFULL (*aside*).

Very pretty, truly. But how the blockhead went out, lan- 290 guishing at her and not a look toward me. Well, churchmen may talk, but miracles are not ceased. For 'tis more than natural, such a rude fellow as he and such a little impertinent as she should be capable of making a woman of my sphere uneasy. But I can bear her sight no longer; methinks she's 295 grown ten times uglier than Cornet. I must go home and study revenge. (*To* Lady Brute.) Madam, your humble servant, I must take my leave.

LADY BRUTE.

What, going already, madam?

LADY FANCYFULL.

I must beg you'll excuse me this once. For really I have 300 eighteen visits to return this afternoon, so you see I'm importuned by the women as well as the men.

BELLINDA (*aside*).

And she's quits with 'em both. (Lady Fancyfull *going*.) Nay, you shan't go one step out of the room.

LADY BRUTE.

Indeed, I'll wait upon you down. 305

LADY FANCYFULL.

No, sweet Lady Brute; you know I swoon at ceremony.

LADY BRUTE.

Pray give me leave.

LADY FANCYFULL.

You know I won't.

LADY BRUTE.

Indeed I must.

296. go] *Q1–2*; *omit Q3, P.*   303. 'em] *Q1–2*; them *Q3, P.*
303. she's] *Q1, P*; she *Q2–3.*

LADY FANCYFULL.

Indeed you shan't.

LADY BRUTE.

Indeed I will.

LADY FANCYFULL.

Indeed you shan't.

LADY BRUTE.

Indeed I will.

LADY FANCYFULL.

Indeed you shan't. Indeed, indeed, indeed you shan't.

Exit Lady Fancyfull *running. They follow.*

Re-enter Lady Brute, *sola.*

LADY BRUTE.

This impertinent woman has put me out of humor for a 315
fortnight. What an agreeable moment has her foolish visit
interrupted. Lord, how like a torrent love flows into the
heart when once the sluice of desire is opened! Good gods,
what a pleasure there is in doing what we should not do!

Re-enter Constant.

Ha! Here again?   320

CONSTANT.

Though the renewing my visit may seem a little irregular,
I hope I shall obtain your pardon for it, madam, when you
know I only left the room lest the lady who was here should
have been as malicious in her remarks as she's foolish in
her conduct.   325

LADY BRUTE.

He who has discretion enough to be tender of a woman's
reputation carries a virtue about him may atone for a great
many faults.

CONSTANT.

If it has a title to atone for any, its pretensions must needs be
strongest where the crime is love. I therefore hope I shall be 330
forgiven the attempt I have made upon your heart, since
my enterprise has been a secret to all the world but yourself.

LADY BRUTE.

Secrecy indeed in sins of this kind is an argument of weight

to lessen the punishment; but nothing's a plea for a pardon
entire, without a sincere repentance.   335

CONSTANT.

If sincerity in repentance consist in sorrow for offending, no
cloister ever enclosed so true a penitent as I should be. But
I hope it cannot be reckoned an offense to love where 'tis a
duty to adore.

LADY BRUTE.

'Tis an offense, a great one, where it would rob a woman of 340
all she ought to be adored for—her virtue.

CONSTANT.

Virtue? Virtue, alas, is no more like the thing that's called
so, than 'tis like vice itself. Virtue consists in goodness, honor,
gratitude, sincerity, and pity, and not in peevish, snarling,
strait-laced chastity. True virtue wheresoe'er it moves still 345
carries an intrinsic worth about it, and is in every place and
in each sex of equal value. So is not continence, you see, that
phantom of honor, which men in every age have so con-
temned, they have thrown it amongst the women to
scrabble for.   350

LADY BRUTE.

If it be a thing of so very little value, why do you so earnestly
recommend it to your wives and daughters?

CONSTANT.

We recommend it to our wives, madam, because we would
keep 'em to ourselves. And to our daughters, because we
would dispose of 'em to others.   355

LADY BRUTE.

'Tis then of some importance, it seems, since you can't
dispose of 'em without it.

CONSTANT.

That importance, madam, lies in the humor of the country,
not in the nature of the thing.

LADY BRUTE.

How do you prove that, sir?   360

CONSTANT.

From the wisdom of a neighboring nation in a contrary
practice. In monarchies things go by whimsy, but common-
wealths weigh all things in the scale of reason.

---

350. *scrabble*] struggle or scramble (for something).

LADY BRUTE.

I hope we are not so very light a people to bring up fashions
without some ground.   365

CONSTANT.

Pray, what does your ladyship think of a powdered coat for
deep mourning?

LADY BRUTE.

I think, sir, your sophistry has all the effect that you can
reasonably expect it should have: it puzzles, but don't
convince.   370

CONSTANT.

I'm sorry for it.

LADY BRUTE.

I'm sorry to hear you say so.

CONSTANT.

Pray why?

LADY BRUTE.

Because if you expected more from it, you have a worse
opinion of my understanding than I desire you should have. 375

CONSTANT (*aside*).

I comprehend her; she would have me set a value upon her
chastity that I may think myself the more obliged to her
when she makes me a present of it. (*To her.*)   I beg you will
believe I did but rally, madam. I know you judge too well of
right and wrong to be deceived by arguments like those. 380
I hope you'll have so favorable an opinion of my understanding, too, to believe the thing called virtue has worth enough
with me to pass for an eternal obligation where'er 'tis
sacrificed.

LADY BRUTE.

It is I think so great a one as nothing can repay.   385

CONSTANT.

Yes, the making the man you love your everlasting debtor.

LADY BRUTE.

When debtors once have borrowed all we have to lend, they
are very apt to grow very shy of their creditors' company.

377. may] *Q1–3*; might *P.*   388. very] *Q1–3*; *omit P.*

364. *bring up*] introduce.

CONSTANT.

That, madam, is only when they are forced to borrow of
usurers and not of a generous friend. Let us choose our 390
creditors, and we are seldom so ungrateful to shun 'em.

LADY BRUTE.

What think you of Sir John, sir? I was his free choice.

CONSTANT.

I think he's married, madam.

LADY BRUTE.

Does marriage then exclude men from your rule of constancy?   395

CONSTANT.

It does. Constancy's a brave, free, haughty, generous agent
that cannot buckle to the chains of wedlock. There's a poor,
sordid slavery in marriage that turns the flowing tide of
honor and sinks us to the lowest ebb of infamy. 'Tis a cor-
rupted soil; ill nature, avarice, sloth, cowardice, and dirt 400
are all its product.

LADY BRUTE.

Have you no exceptions to this general rule, as well as to
t'other?

CONSTANT.

Yes. I would, after all, be an exception to it myself if you
were free in power and will to make me so.   405

LADY BRUTE.

Compliments are well placed where 'tis impossible to lay
hold on 'em.

CONSTANT.

I would to heaven 'twere possible for you to lay hold on
mine, that you might see it is no compliment at all. But since
you are already disposed on beyond redemption to one who 410
does not know the value of the jewel you have put into his
hands, I hope you would not think him greatly wronged,
though it should sometimes be looked on by a friend who
knows how to esteem it as he ought.

LADY BRUTE.

If looking on't alone would serve his turn, the wrong perhaps 415
might not be very great.

410. disposed on] *Q1-3*; disposed
of *P*.

CONSTANT.

Why, what if he should wear it now and then a day, so he
gave good security to bring it home again at night?

LADY BRUTE.

Small security, I fancy, might serve for that. One might
venture to take his word.   420

CONSTANT.

Then where's the injury to the owner?

LADY BRUTE.

'Tis an injury to him if he think it one. For if happiness be
seated in the mind, unhappiness must be so too.

CONSTANT.

Here I close with you, madam, and draw my conclusive
argument from your own position: if the injury lie in the 425
fancy, there needs nothing but secrecy to prevent the wrong.

LADY BRUTE (*going*).

A surer way to prevent it is to hear no more arguments in its
behalf.

CONSTANT (*following her*).

But, madam—

LADY BRUTE.

But, sir, 'tis my turn to be discreet now, and not suffer too 430
long a visit.

CONSTANT (*catching her hand*).

By heaven, you shall not stir, till you give me hopes that I
shall see you again at some more convenient time and place.

LADY BRUTE.

I give you just hopes enough (*breaking from him*) to get loose
from you. And that's all I can afford you at this time.   435

Exit running

CONSTANT (*solus*).

Now by all that's great and good, she is a charming
woman! In what ecstasy of joy she has left me! For she gave
me hope; did she not say she gave me hope? Hope? Aye,
what hope? Enough to make me let her go. Why that's
enough in conscience. Or no matter how 'twas spoke. Hope 440
was the word; it came from her and it was said to me.

Enter Heartfree.

Ha, Heartfree, thou hast done me noble service in prattling

–55–

to the young gentlewoman without there; come to my arms,
thou venerable bawd, and let me squeeze thee (*embracing
him eagerly*) as a new pair of stays does a fat country girl   445
when she's carried to court to stand for a maid of honor.

HEARTFREE.

Why, what the devil's all this rapture for?

CONSTANT.

Rapture? There's ground for rapture, man, there's hopes,
my Heartfree, hopes, my friend!

HEARTFREE.

Hopes? Of what?   450

CONSTANT.

Why, hopes that my lady and I together—for 'tis more than
one body's work—should make Sir John a cuckold.

HEARTFREE.

Prithee, what did she say to thee?

CONSTANT.

Say? What did she not say? She said that—says she—she
said—zounds I don't know what she said; but she looked as   455
if she said everything I'd have her, and so if thou'lt go to the
tavern I'll treat thee with anything that gold can buy. I'll
give all my silver amongst the drawers, make a bonfire
before the door, say the plenipos have signed the peace,
and the Bank of England's grown honest.   *Exeunt.* 460

[III.ii]   [*The Blue Posts Tavern.*]
Scene opens. Lord Rake, [Colonel Bully], Sir John, *etc., at a table drinking.*

ALL.

Huzza.

LORD RAKE.

Come boys! Charge again! So. Confusion to all order.
Here's liberty of conscience.

ALL.

Huzza.

LORD RAKE.

I'll sing you a song I made this morning to this purpose.   5

---

459. *signed the peace*] The Treaty of Ryswick, ending the war that England had been engaged in since 1689, was not signed until September, 1697,
but peace had been expected for the past year.

460. *Bank of England*] Founded in 1694 and opposed by Tory-sponsored
land banks, the Bank of England was not yet above suspicion.

SIR JOHN.

    'Tis wicked, I hope.

COLONEL BULLY.

    Don't my lord tell you he made it?

SIR JOHN.

    Well then, let's ha't.

LORD RAKE (*sings*).

I

    What a pother of late

    Have they kept in the state   10

        About setting our consciences free.

    A bottle has more

    Dispensation in store,

        Than the king and the state can decree.

II

    When my head's full of wine,   15

    I o'erflow with design

        And know no penal laws that can curb me.

    Whate'er I devise

    Seems good in my eyes,

        And religion ne'er dares to disturb me.   20

III

    No saucy remorse

    Intrudes in my course,

        Nor impertinent notions of evil.

    So there's claret in store,

    In peace I've my whore,   25

        And in peace I jog on to the devil.

9–28. For the song that ultimately displaced this one on the stage, see Appendix A.

11. *setting . . . free*] The reference is vaguely to the Toleration Act of 1689; liberty of conscience remained topical throughout the reigns of William III and Anne.

13. *Dispensation*] the power claimed by Charles II and James II to suspend penalties of the law in individual cases; it was particluarly used by James II to allow Catholics to hold office.

17. *penal laws*] The severe penal laws against practicing the Roman Catholic religion (although not repealed until 1778) were not usually enforced in England. But at this time increasingly severe laws were being imposed on Catholics in Ireland, so that the issue was very much alive.

ALL *(sing)*.

> So there's claret, etc.

LORD RAKE *(repeats)*.

> And in peace I jog on to the devil.

> Well, how do you like it, gentlemen?

ALL.

> O, admirable.   30

SIR JOHN.

> I would not give a fig for a song that is not full of sin and
> impudence.

LORD RAKE.

> Then my muse is to your taste. But drink away; the night
> steals upon us, we shall want time to be lewd in. Hey, Page,
> sally out, sirrah, and see what's doing in the camp. We'll   35
> beat up their quarters presently.

PAGE.

> I'll bring your lordship an exact account.   *Exit* Page.

LORD RAKE.

> Now let the spirit of clary go round. Fill me a brimmer.
> Here's to our forlorn hope. Courage, knight, victory attends
> you.   40

SIR JOHN.

> And laurels shall crown me. Drink away and be damned.

LORD RAKE.

> Again, boys. T'other glass, and damn morality.

SIR JOHN *(drunk)*.

> Aye—damn morality—and damn the watch. And let the
> constable be married.

ALL.

> Huzza.   45

> *Re-enter* Page.

LORD RAKE.

> How are the streets inhabited, sirrah?

---

36. *beat . . . quarters*] arouse or disturb by an unexpected visit. The
phrase was military in origin but came to be used for unseasonable and
violent visits to houses of prostitution; cf. Rochester, "The Maimed
Debauchee": ". . . Bawds quarters beaten up, and Fortress won;/ Windows
demolish'd, Watches overcome. . . ."

38. *clary*] a wine drink with honey and spices.

PAGE.

My lord, it's Sunday night, they are full of drunken citizens.

LORD RAKE.

Along then, boys, we shall have a feast.

COLONEL BULLY.

Along, noble knight.

SIR JOHN.

Aye. Along, Bully. And he that says Sir John Brute is not as 50
drunk and as religious as the drunkenest citizen of 'em all—
is a liar, and the son of a whore.

COLONEL BULLY.

Why, that was bravely spoke, and like a free-born Englishman.

SIR JOHN.

What's that to you, sir, whether I am an Englishman or a 55
Frenchman?

COLONEL BULLY.

Zounds, you are not angry, sir?

SIR JOHN.

Zounds, I am angry, sir—for if I am a free-born Englishman,
what have you to do even to talk of my privileges?

LORD RAKE.

Why prithee, knight, don't quarrel here; leave private 60
animosities to be decided by daylight, let the night be
employed against the public enemy.

SIR JOHN.

My lord, I respect you, because you are a man of quality.
But I'll make that fellow know I am within a hairsbreadth
as absolute by my privileges as the King of France is by his 65
prerogative. He by his prerogative takes money where it is
not his due; I, by my privilege refuse paying it where I owe
it. Liberty and property and Old England, huzza.

ALL.

Huzza.   *Exit Sir John reeling, all following him.*

[III.iii]   *A bedchamber.*
                        Enter Lady Brute *and* Bellinda.

LADY BRUTE.

Sure it's late, Bellinda? I begin to be sleepy.

BELLINDA.

Yes, 'tis near twelve. Will you go to bed?

LADY BRUTE.

To bed, my dear? And by that time I'm fallen into a sweet sleep (or perhaps a sweet dream, which is better and better), Sir John will come home roaring drunk, and be 5 overjoyed he finds me in a condition to be disturbed.

BELLINDA.

O, you need not fear him, he's in for all night. The servants say he's gone to drink with my Lord Rake.

LADY BRUTE.

Nay, 'tis not very likely indeed such suitable company should part presently. What hogs men turn, Bellinda, when 10 they grow weary of women.

BELLINDA.

And what owls they are whilst they are fond of 'em.

LADY BRUTE.

But that we may forgive well enough, because they are so upon our accounts.

BELLINDA.

We ought to do so indeed. But 'tis a hard matter. For when 15 a man is really in love, he looks so unsufferably silly that though a woman liked him well enough before, she has then much ado to endure the sight of him. And this I take to be the reason why lovers are so generally ill used.

LADY BRUTE.

Well I own now, I'm well enough pleased to see a man 20 look like an ass for me.

BELLINDA.

Aye, I'm pleased he should look like an ass too—that is, I'm pleased with myself for making him look so.

LADY BRUTE.

Nay truly, I think if he'd find some other way to express his passion, 'twould be more to his advantage. 25

BELLINDA.

Yes, for then a woman might like his passion and him too.

LADY BRUTE.

Yet, Bellinda, after all, a woman's life would be but a dull business if 'twere not for men—and men that can look like asses too. We should never blame fate for the shortness of our days; our time would hang wretchedly upon our hands.　30

BELLINDA.

Why truly, they do help us off with a good share on't. For
were there no men in the world, o' my conscience I should
be no longer a-dressing than I'm a-saying my prayers, nay
though it were Sunday; for you know that one may go to
church without stays on.　35

LADY BRUTE.

But don't you think emulation might do something? For
every woman you see desires to be finer than her neighbor.

BELLINDA.

That's only that the men may like her better than her neighbor. No, if there were no men, adieu fine petticoats, we
should be weary of wearing 'em.　40

LADY BRUTE.

And adieu plays, we should be weary of seeing 'em.

BELLINDA.

Adieu Hyde Park, the dust would choke us.

LADY BRUTE.

Adieu St. James's, walking would tire us.

BELLINDA.

Adieu London, the smoke would stifle us.

LADY BRUTE.

And adieu going to church, for religion would ne'er prevail　45
with us.

BOTH.

Ha ha ha ha ha!

BELLINDA.

Our confession is so very hearty, sure we merit absolution.

LADY BRUTE.

Not unless we go through with't and confess all. So prithee,
for the ease of our consciences, let's hide nothing.　50

BELLINDA.

Agreed.

LADY BRUTE.

Why then I confess that I love to sit in the forefront of a box.
For if one sits behind, there's two acts gone perhaps before
one's found out. And when I am there, if I perceive the

34. know that] *Q1–3*; know *P*.

men whispering and looking upon me, you must know I   55
cannot for my life forbear thinking, they talk to my advantage. And that sets a thousand little tickling vanities on
foot.

BELLINDA.

Just my case for all the world; but go on.

LADY BRUTE.

I watch with impatience for the next jest in the play, that I   60
may laugh and show my white teeth. If the poet has been
dull and the jest be long a-coming, I pretend to whisper one
to my friend, and from thence fall into a little short discourse
in which I take occasion to show my face in all humors,
brisk, pleased, serious, melancholy, languishing. Not that   65
what we say to one another causes any of these alterations.
But—

BELLINDA.

Don't trouble yourself to explain; for if I'm not mistaken,
you and I have had some of these necessary dialogues before
now with the same intention.   70

LADY BRUTE.

Why I'll swear, Bellinda, some people do give strange
agreeable airs to their faces in speaking. Tell me true, did
you never practice in the glass?

BELLINDA.

Why, did you?

LADY BRUTE.

Yes faith, many a time.   75

BELLINDA.

And I too, I own it. Both how to speak myself and how to
look when others speak. But my glass and I could never yet
agree what face I should make when they come blurt out
with a nasty thing in a play. For all the men presently look
upon the women, that's certain; so laugh we must not,   80
though our stays burst for it, because that's telling truth and
owning we understand the jest. And to look serious is so dull,
when the whole house is a-laughing.

LADY BRUTE.

Besides, that looking serious does really betray our knowl-

61. may] *Q1–3*; might *P*.   63. short] *Q1*; small *Q2–3, P*.

edge in the matter as much as laughing with the company   85
would do; for if we did not understand the thing we should
naturally do like other people.

BELLINDA.

For my part, I always take that occasion to blow my nose.

LADY BRUTE.

You must blow your nose half off then at some plays.

BELLINDA.

Why don't some reformer or other beat the poet for't?   90

LADY BRUTE.

Because he is not so sure of our private approbation as of
our public thanks. Well, sure there is not upon earth so
impertinent a thing as women's modesty.

BELLINDA.

Yes, men's fantasque, that obliges us to it. If we quit our
modesty they say we lose our charms, and yet they know   95
that very modesty is affectation and rail at our hypocrisy.

LADY BRUTE.

Thus one would think 'twere a hard matter to please 'em,
niece. Yet our kind Mother Nature has given us something
that makes amends for all. Let our weakness be what it will,
mankind will still be weaker, and whilst there is a world, 100
'tis woman that will govern it. But prithee, one word of
poor Constant before we go to bed, if it be but to furnish
matter for dreams; I dare swear he's talking of me now, or
thinking of me at least, though it be in the middle of his
prayers.   105

BELLINDA.

So he ought, I think; for you were pleased to make him a
good round advance today, madam.

LADY BRUTE.

Why, I have e'en plagued him enough to satisfy any
reasonable woman. He has besieged me these two years to
no purpose.   110

BELLINDA.

And if he besieged you two years more, he'd be well
enough paid, so he had the plundering of you at last.

---

90. *reformer . . . poet*] Like the reference to a "venomed priest" in the
Prologue, this foreshadows Collier's attack on the morality of the stage.
94. *fantasque*] fancy, whim.

LADY BRUTE.

> That may be. But I'm afraid the town won't be able to hold
> out much longer; for to confess the truth to you, Bellinda,
> the garrison begins to grow mutinous.　　　　　115

BELLINDA.

> Then the sooner you capitulate, the better.

LADY BRUTE.

> Yet methinks I would fain stay a little longer, to see you
> fixed too, that we might start together and see who could
> love longest. What think you if Heartfree should have a
> month's mind to you?　　　　　120

BELLINDA.

> Why faith, I could almost be in love with him for despising
> that foolish affected Lady Fancyfull, but I'm afraid he's too
> cold ever to warm himself by my fire.

LADY BRUTE.

> Then he deserves to be froze to death. Would I were a man
> for your sake, my dear rogue.　　　　　*Kissing her.*　125

BELLINDA.

> You'd wish yourself a woman again for your own, or the
> men are mistaken. But if I could make a conquest of this son
> of Bacchus and rival his bottle, what should I do with him?
> He has no fortune; I can't marry him, and sure you would
> not have me commit fornication.　　　　　130

LADY BRUTE.

> Why, if you did, child, 'twould be but a good friendly part,
> if 'twere only to keep me in countenance whilst I commit—
> you know what.

BELLINDA.

> Well, if I can't resolve to serve you that way, I may perhaps
> some other, as much to your satisfaction. But pray, how　135
> shall we contrive to see these blades again quickly?

LADY BRUTE.

> We must e'en have recourse to the old way: make 'em an
> appointment 'twixt jest and earnest, 'twill look like a frolic,
> and that you know's a very good thing to save a woman's
> blushes.　　　　　140

125. my] *Q1–3; omit P.*

---

120. *month's mind*] strong inclination.

BELLINDA.

You advise well; but where shall it be?

LADY BRUTE.

In Spring Garden. But they shan't know their women till
their women pull off their masques, for a surprise is the most
agreeable thing in the world. And I find myself in a very
good humor, ready to do 'em any good turn I can think on.   145

BELLINDA.

Then pray write 'em the necessary billet without farther
delay.

LADY BRUTE.

Let's go into your chamber then, and whilst you say your
prayers I'll do it, child.   *Exeunt.*

---

142. *Spring Garden*] The original Spring Garden near Charing Cross in
the 1660's gave way to a new Spring Garden in Lambeth, later to be called
Vauxhall. Tom Brown's description dates from about the time of this play:
"The ladies that have an inclination to be private take delight in the close
walks of Spring Gardens, where both sexes meet and mutually serve one
another as guides to lose their way; and the windings and turnings in the
little wildernesses are so intricate that the most experienced mothers have
oft lost themselves in looking for their daughters." See also *The Spectator*,
No. 383.

ACT IV

[IV.i]   *Covent Garden.*
                Enter Lord Rake, Sir John, *etc., with swords drawn.*

LORD RAKE.

Is the dog dead?

COLONEL BULLY.

No, damn him, I heard him wheeze.

LORD RAKE.

How the witch his wife howled!

COLONEL BULLY.

Aye, she'll alarm the watch presently.

LORD RAKE.

Appear, knight, then. Come you have a good cause to fight   5
for, there's a man murdered.

SIR JOHN.

Is there? Then let his ghost be satisfied; for I'll sacrifice a
constable to it presently, and burn his body upon his wooden
chair.

                Enter a Tailor *with a bundle under his arm.*

COLONEL BULLY.

How now? What have we got here, a thief?   10

TAILOR.

No, an't please you. I'm no thief.

LORD RAKE.

That we'll see presently. Here, let the general examine him.

SIR JOHN.

Aye, aye. Let me examine him, and I'll lay a hundred
pound I find him guilty in spite of his teeth, for he looks—
like a—sneaking rascal. Come sirrah, without equivocation   15
or mental reservation, tell me of what opinion you are and
what calling, for by them—I shall guess at your morals.

TAILOR.

An't please you, I'm a dissenting journeyman tailor.

SIR JOHN.

Then sirrah, you love lying by your religion, and theft by
your trade. And so that your punishment may be suitable   20

IV.i] For a revision of this scene, see Appendix B.

to your crimes, I'll have you first gagged, and then hanged.

TAILOR.

Pray good worthy gentlemen, don't abuse me; indeed I'm an honest man and a good workman, though I say it that should not say it.   25

SIR JOHN.

No words, sirrah, but attend your fate.

LORD RAKE.

Let me see what's in that bundle.

TAILOR.

An't please you, it's the doctor of the parish's gown.

LORD RAKE.

The doctor's gown! Hark you, knight, you won't stick at abusing the clergy, will you?   30

SIR JOHN.

No, I'm drunk, and I'll abuse anything—but my wife: and her I name—with reverence.

LORD RAKE.

Then you shall wear this gown whilst you charge the watch, that though the blows fall upon you, the scandal may light upon the church.   35

SIR JOHN.

A generous design, by all the gods; give it me.

Takes the gown and puts it on.

TAILOR.

O dear gentlemen, I shall be quite undone if you take the gown.

SIR JOHN.

Retire, sirrah. And since you carry off your skin, go home and be happy.   40

TAILOR (*pausing*).

I think I had e'en as good follow the gentleman's friendly advice. For if I dispute any longer, who knows but the whim may take him to case me. These courtiers are fuller of tricks than they are of money; they'll sooner cut a man's throat than pay his bill.   *Exit* Tailor.   45

28. it's] *Q1–3*; it is *P*.

---

43. *case*] strip the skin from.

SIR JOHN.

So, how d'ye like my shapes now?

LORD RAKE.

This will do to a miracle; he looks like a bishop going to the
Holy War. But to your arms, gentlemen, the enemy appears.

Enter Constable *and* Watch.

WATCHMAN.

Stand! Who goes there? Come before the constable.

SIR JOHN.

The constable's a rascal—and you are the son of a whore.   50

WATCHMAN.

A good civil answer for a parson, truly.

CONSTABLE.

Methinks, sir, a man of your coat might set a better example.

SIR JOHN.

Sirrah, I'll make you know—there are men of my coat can
set as bad examples—as you can do, you dog you.

Sir John *strikes the* Constable. *They knock him down, disarm him and seize
him.* Lord Rake, *etc., run away.*

CONSTABLE.

So, we have secured the parson however.   55

SIR JOHN.

Blood and blood—and blood.

WATCHMAN.

Lord have mercy upon us. How the wicked wretch raves of
blood. I'll warrant he has been murdering somebody tonight.

SIR JOHN.

Sirrah, there's nothing got by murder but a halter; my
talent lies towards drunkenness and simony.   60

WATCHMAN.

Why that now was spoke like a man of parts, neighbors; it's
pity he should be so disguised.

SIR JOHN.

You lie. I am not disguised, for I am drunk barefaced.

WATCHMAN.

Look you there again. This is a mad parson, Mr. Constable; I'll lay a pot of ale upon's head he's a good preacher.   65

63. I am not] *Q1–3*; I'm not *P.*

CONSTABLE.

Come sir, out of respect to your calling I shan't put you into
the roundhouse, but we must secure you in our drawing-
room till morning, that you may do no mischief. So, come
along.

SIR JOHN.

You may put me where you will, sirrah, now you have over-   70
come me. But if I can't do mischief I'll think of mischief—in
spite of your teeth, you dog you.   *Exeunt.*

[IV.ii]   *A bedchamber.*
                          Enter Heartfree, *solus.*

HEARTFREE.

What the plague ails me? Love? No, I thank you for that;
my heart's rock still. Yet 'tis Bellinda that disturbs me,
that's positive. Well, what of all that? Must I love her for
being troublesome? At that rate, I might love all the
women I meet, I gad. But hold! Though I don't love her   5
for disturbing me, yet she may disturb me because I love her.
Aye, that may be, faith. I have dreamt of her, that's
certain. Well, so I have of my mother; therefore what's that
to the purpose? Aye, but Bellinda runs in my mind waking.
And so does many a damned thing that I don't care a   10
farthing for. Methinks, though, I would fain be talking to
her, and yet I have no business. Well, am I the first man
that has had a mind to do an impertinent thing?

                          Enter Constant.

CONSTANT.

How now, Heartfree? What makes you up and dressed
so soon? I thought none but lovers quarreled with their   15
beds; I expected to have found you snoring, as I used to do.

HEARTFREE.

Why faith, friend, 'tis the care I have of your affairs that
makes me so thoughtful; I have been studying all night how
to bring your matter about with Bellinda.

CONSTANT.

With Bellinda?   20

---

67. *roundhouse*] a constable's lock-up.

HEARTFREE.

> With my lady, I mean. And faith, I have mighty hopes
> on't. Sure you must be very well satisfied with her behavior
> to you yesterday.

CONSTANT.

> So well, that nothing but a lover's fears can make me doubt
> of success. But what can this sudden change proceed from?   25

HEARTFREE.

> Why, you saw her husband beat her, did you not?

CONSTANT.

> That's true; a husband is scarce to be borne upon any terms,
> much less when he fights with his wife. Methinks she should
> e'en have cuckolded him upon the very spot, to show that
> after the battle she was master of the field.   30

HEARTFREE.

> A council of war of women would infallibly have advised her
> to't. But, I confess, so agreeable a woman as Bellinda
> deserves a better usage.

CONSTANT.

> Bellinda again?

HEARTFREE.

> My lady, I mean. What a pox makes me blunder so today?   35
> (*Aside.*)   A plague of this treacherous tongue.

CONSTANT.

> Prithee look upon me seriously, Heartfree. Now answer me
> directly. Is it my lady, or Bellinda, employs your careful
> thoughts thus?

HEARTFREE.

> My lady, or Bellinda?   40

CONSTANT.

> In love, by this light in love!

HEARTFREE.

> In love?

CONSTANT.

> Nay, ne'er deny it, for thou'lt do it so awkwardly 'twill but
> make the jest sit heavier about thee. My dear friend, I give
> thee much joy.   45

HEARTFREE.

> Why prithee, you won't persuade me to it, will you?

CONSTANT.

> That she's mistress of your tongue, that's plain, and I know

you are so honest a fellow, your tongue and heart always go
together. But how? But how the devil? Pha, ha, ha, ha—

HEARTFREE.

Hey-day! Why sure you don't believe it in earnest?   50

CONSTANT.

Yes, I do, because I see you deny it in jest.

HEARTFREE.

Nay, but look you, Ned—a—deny in jest—a—gadzooks,
you know I say—a—when a man denies a thing in jest—a—

CONSTANT.

Pha, ha, ha, ha, ha!

HEARTFREE.

Nay then we shall have it. What, because a man stumbles at   55
a word? Did you never make a blunder?

CONSTANT.

Yes, for I am in love; I own it.

HEARTFREE.

Then, so am I. (*Embracing him.*)   Now laugh till thy
soul's glutted with mirth; but, dear Constant, don't tell the
town on't.   60

CONSTANT.

Nay, then 'twere almost pity to laugh at thee, after so
honest a confession. But tell us a little, Jack. By what new-
invented arms has this mighty stroke been given?

HEARTFREE.

E'en by that unaccountable weapon called, *je ne sais quoi*;
for everything that can come within the verge of beauty, I   65
have seen it with indifference.

CONSTANT.

So in few words then, the *je ne sais quoi* has been too hard for
the quilted petticoat.

HEARTFREE.

Egad, I think the *je ne sais quoi* is in the quilted petticoat; at
least, 'tis certain I ne'er think on't without—a—a *je ne sais*   70
quoi in every part about me.

CONSTANT.

Well, but have all your remedies lost their virtue? Have you
turned her inside-out yet?

---

64. *je ne sais quoi*] I know not what—an attraction that cannot be explained.

HEARTFREE.

I dare not so much as think on't.

CONSTANT.

But don't the two years' fatigue I have had discourage you?   75

HEARTFREE.

Yes, I dread what I foresee, yet cannot quit the enterprise.
Like some soldiers whose courage dwells more in their honor
than their nature, on they go, though the body trembles at
what the soul makes it undertake.

CONSTANT.

Nay, if you expect your mistress will use you as your pro-   80
fanations against her sex deserve, you tremble justly. But
how do you intend to proceed, friend?

HEARTFREE.

Thou know'st I'm but a novice; be friendly and advise me.

CONSTANT.

Why look you then, I'd have you—serenade and a—write
a song—go to church, look like a fool, be very officious, ogle,   85
write, and lead out; and who knows, but in a year or two's
time you may be—called a troublesome puppy and sent
about your business.

HEARTFREE.

That's hard.

CONSTANT.

Yet thus it oft falls out with lovers, sir.   90

HEARTFREE.

Pox on me for making one of the number.

CONSTANT.

Have a care. Say no saucy things. 'Twill but augment your
crime, and if your mistress hears on't increase your punishment.

HEARTFREE.

Prithee say something then to encourage me; you know I   95
helped you in your distress.

CONSTANT.

Why then to encourage you to perseverance, that you may be
thoroughly ill used for your offenses, I'll put you in mind that
even the coyest ladies of 'em all are made up of desires as well

---

86. *lead out*] possibly with reference to leading out in a card game.

as we, and though they do hold out a long time they will 100
capitulate at last. For that thundering engineer, nature,
does make such havoc in the town, they must surrender at
long run or perish in their own flames.

Enter a Footman.

[FOOTMAN.]

Sir, there's a porter without with a letter; he desires to give
it into your own hands.   105

CONSTANT.

Call him in.   [*Exit* Footman.]

Enter Porter.

What, Jo, is it thee?

PORTER.

An't please you sir, I was ordered to deliver this into your
own hands, by two well-shaped ladies at the New Exchange.
I was at your honor's lodgings, and your servants sent me 110
hither.

CONSTANT.

'Tis well. Are you to carry any answer?

PORTER.

No, my noble master. They gave me my orders, and whip,
they were gone, like a maidenhead at fifteen.

CONSTANT.

Very well. There.   *Gives him money.* 115

PORTER.

God bless your honor.   *Exit* Porter.

CONSTANT.

Now let's see what honest trusty Jo has brought us.—(*Reads.*)
"If you and your playfellow can spare time from your
business and devotions, don't fail to be at Spring Garden
about eight in the evening. You'll find nothing there but 120
women, so you need bring no other arms than what you
usually carry about you."—So, playfellow, here's something
to stay your stomach till your mistress's dish is ready for you.

---

109. *New Exchange*] an arcade on the south side of the Strand with small
novelty shops and lodgings. The third acts of both Etherege's *She Would if
She Could* and Wycherley's *The Country Wife* have good descriptions of its
activities.

HEARTFREE.

    Some of our old battered acquaintance. I won't go, not I.

CONSTANT.

    Nay, that you can't avoid. There's honor in the case; 'tis a   125
challenge and I want a second.

HEARTFREE.

    I doubt I shall be but a very useless one to you; for I'm so
disheartened by this wound Bellinda has given me, I don't
think I shall have courage enough to draw my sword.

CONSTANT.

    O, if that be all, come along. I'll warrant you find sword   130
enough for such enemies as we have to deal withal.   *Exeunt.*

[IV.iii]   *[A street.]*
Enter Constable, *etc., with* Sir John.

CONSTABLE.

    Come along, sir. I thought to have let you slip this morning
because you were a minister, but you are as drunk and as
abusive as ever. We'll see what the Justice of the Peace will
say to you.

SIR JOHN.

    And you shall see what I'll say to the Justice of the Peace,   5
sirrah.   *They knock at the door.*

Enter Servant.

CONSTABLE.

    Pray acquaint his worship, we have got an unruly parson
here. We are unwilling to expose him, but don't know what
to do with him.

SERVANT.

    I'll acquaint my master.   *Exit* Servant.   10

SIR JOHN.

    You, Constable, what damned Justice is this?

CONSTABLE.

    One that will take care of you, I warrant you.

Enter Justice.

JUSTICE.

    Well, Mr. Constable, what's the disorder here?

IV.iii.] For a revision of this scene, see Appendix B.

CONSTABLE.

>An't please your worship—

SIR JOHN.

>Let me speak and be damned; I'm a divine and can unfold   15
>mysteries better than you can do.

JUSTICE.

>Sadness, sadness, a minister so overtaken. Pray sir, give the
>constable leave to speak, and I'll hear you very patiently;
>I assure you, sir, I will.

SIR JOHN.

>Sir, you are a very civil magistrate. Your most humble   20
>servant.

CONSTABLE.

>An't please your worship then, he has attempted to beat the
>watch tonight, and swore—

SIR JOHN.

>You lie.

JUSTICE.

>Hold, pray sir, a little.   25

SIR JOHN.

>Sir, your very humble servant.

CONSTABLE.

>Indeed sir, he came at us without any provocation, called
>us whores and rogues, and laid us on with a great quarter-
>staff. He was in my Lord Rake's company. They have been
>playing the devil tonight.   30

JUSTICE.

>Hem, hem. Pray sir, may you be chaplain to my lord?

SIR JOHN.

>Sir, I presume—I may if I will.

JUSTICE.

>My meaning, sir, is, are you so?

SIR JOHN.

>Sir, you mean very well.

JUSTICE.

>He hem, hem. Under favor, sir, pray answer me directly.   35

SIR JOHN.

>Under favor, sir, do you use to answer directly when you
>are drunk?

4

JUSTICE.

Good lack, good lack. Here's nothing to be got from him.
Pray sir, may I crave your name?

SIR JOHN.

Sir, my name's—(*he hiccups*) Hiccup, sir.   40

JUSTICE.

Hiccup? Doctor Hiccup. I have known a great many
country parsons of that name, especially down in the fens.
Pray where do you live, sir?

SIR JOHN.

Here—and there, sir.

JUSTICE.

Why, what a strange man is this? Where do you preach, sir?   45
Have you any cure?

SIR JOHN.

Sir—I have—a very good cure—for a clap, at your service.

JUSTICE.

Lord have mercy upon us.

SIR JOHN (*aside*).

This fellow does ask so many impertinent questions, I
believe, egad, 'tis the Justice's wife in the Justice's clothes.   50

JUSTICE.

Mr. Constable, I vow and protest, I don't know what to do
with him.

CONSTABLE.

Truly he has been but a troublesome guest to us all night.

JUSTICE.

I think I had e'en best let him go about his business, for I'm
unwilling to expose him.   55

CONSTABLE.

E'en what your worship thinks fit.

SIR JOHN.

Sir, not to interrupt Mr. Constable, I have a small favor to
ask.

JUSTICE.

Sir, I open both my ears to you.

SIR JOHN.

Sir, your very humble servant. I have a little urgent   60
business calls upon me, and therefore I desire the favor of
you to bring matters to a conclusion.

JUSTICE.

Sir, if I were sure that business were not to commit more
disorders, I would release you.

SIR JOHN.

None, by my priesthood.   65

JUSTICE.

Then, Mr. Constable, you may discharge him.

SIR JOHN.

Sir, your very humble servant. If you please to accept of a
bottle—

JUSTICE.

I thank you kindly, sir, but I never drink in a morning.
Goodby to ye, sir, goodby to ye.   70

SIR JOHN.

Goodby t'ye, good sir.   *Exit* Justice.
So, now, Mr. Constable, shall you and I go pick up a whore
together?

CONSTABLE.

No, thank you, sir; my wife's enough to satisfy any reasonable man.   75

SIR JOHN (*aside*).

He, he, he, he, he! The fool is married, then. Well, you
won't go?

CONSTABLE.

Not I, truly.

SIR JOHN.

Then I'll go by myself; and you and your wife may be
damned.   *Exit* Sir John. 80

CONSTABLE (*gazing after him*).

Why, God a-mercy, parson.   *Exeunt.*

[IV.iv]   *Spring Garden.*

Constant *and* Heartfree *cross the stage. As they go off, enter* Lady Fancyfull *and* Madamoiselle, *masked and dogging 'em.*

CONSTANT.

So, I think we are about the time appointed; let us walk up
this way.   *Exeunt.*

LADY FANCYFULL.

Good. Thus far I have dogged 'em without being discovered. 'Tis infallibly some intrigue that brings them to

Spring Garden. How my poor heart is torn and racked with   5
fear and jealousy. Yet let it be anything but that flirt
Bellinda and I'll try to bear it. But if it prove her, all that's
woman in me shall be employed to destroy her.

Exeunt after Constant *and* Heartfree.

Reenter Constant *and* Heartfree, Lady Fancyfull *and* Madamoiselle
still following at a distance.

CONSTANT.

I see no females yet that have anything to say to us. I'm
afraid we are bantered.   10

HEARTFREE.

I wish we were, for I'm in no humor to make either them or
myself merry.

CONSTANT.

Nay, I'm sure you'll make them merry enough if I tell 'em
why you are dull. But prithee, why so heavy and sad before
you begin to be ill-used?   15

HEARTFREE.

For the same reason, perhaps, that you are so brisk and well
pleased; because both pains and pleasures are generally more
considerable in prospect than when they come to pass.

Enter Lady Brute *and* Bellinda, *masked and poorly dressed.*

CONSTANT.

How now, who are these? Not our game, I hope.

HEARTFREE.

If they are, we are e'en well enough served, to come hunting   20
here when we had so much better game in chase elsewhere.

LADY FANCYFULL (*to* Madamoiselle).

So, those are their ladies, without doubt. But I'm afraid that
doily stuff is not worn for want of better clothes. They are the
very shape and size of Bellinda and her aunt.

MADAMOISELLE.

So day be inteed, matam.   25

20. hunting] *Q 1–3*; a hunting *P.*

---

23. *doily*] light-weight woolen material devised by Thomas Doyly "who
raised a fortune by finding out materials for such stuffs as might at once be
cheap and genteel" (*The Spectator,* No. 283).

LADY FANCYFULL.

We'll slip into this close arbor, where we may hear all they
say.   *Exeunt* Lady Fancyfull *and* Madamoiselle.

LADY BRUTE.

What, are you afraid of us, gentlemen?

HEARTFREE.

Why, truly I think we may, if appearance don't lie.

BELLINDA.

Do you always find women what they appear to be, sir?   30

HEARTFREE.

No forsooth; but I seldom find 'em better than they appear
to be.

BELLINDA.

Then the outside's best, you think?

HEARTFREE.

'Tis the honestest.

CONSTANT.

Have a care, Heartfree; you are relapsing again.   35

LADY BRUTE.

Why, does the gentleman use to rail at women?

CONSTANT.

He has done formerly.

BELLINDA.

I suppose he had very good cause for't: they did not use you
so well as you thought you deserved, sir.

LADY BRUTE.

They made themselves merry at your expense, sir.   40

BELLINDA.

Laughed when you sighed.

LADY BRUTE.

Slept while you were waking.

BELLINDA.

Had your porter beat.

LADY BRUTE.

And threw your billet-doux in the fire?

HEARTFREE.

Hey-day, I shall do more than rail presently.   45

BELLINDA.

Why, you won't beat us, will you?

HEARTFREE.

I don't know but I may.

CONSTANT.

What the devil's coming here? Sir John in a gown? And drunk, i'faith.

Enter Sir John.

SIR JOHN.

What a pox! Here's Constant, Heartfree, and two whores,   50
egad. O you covetous rogues; what have you never a spare
punk for your friend? But I'll share with you.

He seizes both the women.

HEARTFREE.

Why, what the plague have you been doing, knight?

SIR JOHN.

Why, I have been beating the watch and scandalizing the
clergy.   55

HEARTFREE.

A very good account, truly.

SIR JOHN.

And what do you think I'll do next?

CONSTANT.

Nay, that no man can guess.

SIR JOHN.

Why, if you'll let me sup with you, I'll treat both your
strumpets.   60

LADY BRUTE *(aside)*.

O Lord, we are undone.

HEARTFREE.

No, we can't sup together, because we have some affairs
elsewhere. But if you'll accept of these two ladies, we'll be so
complaisant to you to resign our right in 'em.

BELLINDA *(aside)*.

Lord, what shall we do?   65

SIR JOHN.

Let me see, their clothes are such damned clothes they won't
pawn for the reckoning.

HEARTFREE.

Sir John, your servant. Rapture attend you.

CONSTANT.

Adieu, ladies. Make much of the gentleman.

LADY BRUTE.

Why sure, you won't leave us in the hands of a drunken   70
fellow to abuse us?

SIR JOHN.

> Who do you call a drunken fellow, you slut you? I'm a man
> of quality; the king has made me a knight.

HEARTFREE.

> Aye, aye, you are in good hands, adieu, adieu.

Heartfree runs off.

LADY BRUTE.

> The devil's hands. Let me go, or I'll—For heaven's sake   75
> protect us.

She breaks from him, runs to Constant, *twitching off her mask and clapping
it on again.*

SIR JOHN.

> I'll devil you, you jade you. I'll demolish your ugly face.

CONSTANT.

> Hold a little, knight; she swoons.

SIR JOHN.

> I'll swoon her.

CONSTANT.

> Hey, Heartfree.   80

Reenter Heartfree. Bellinda *runs to him and shows her face.*

HEARTFREE.

> O heavens! My dear creature, stand there a little.

CONSTANT.

> Pull him off, Jack.

HEARTFREE.

> Hold, mighty man. Look you, sir, we did but jest with you.
> These are ladies of our acquaintance that we had a mind to
> frighten a little. But now you must leave us.   85

SIR JOHN.

> Oons, I won't leave you, not I.

HEARTFREE.

> Nay, but you must though; and therefore make no words
> on't.

SIR JOHN.

> Then you are a couple of damned uncivil fellows. And I
> hope your punks will give you sauce to your mutton.   90

Exit Sir John.

---

90. *sauce*] here, venereal disease.   90. *mutton*] prostitute.

LADY BRUTE.

O, I shall never come to myself again, I'm so frightened.

CONSTANT.

'Twas a narrow scape indeed.

BELLINDA.

Women must have frolics, you see, whatever they cost 'em.

HEARTFREE.

This might have proved a dear one, though.

LADY BRUTE.

You are the more obliged to us for the risk we run upon your   95
accounts.

CONSTANT.

And I hope you'll acknowledge something due to our knight
errantry, ladies. This is the second time we have delivered
you.

LADY BRUTE.

'Tis true; and since we see fate has designed you for our guar-   100
dians, 'twill make us the more willing to trust ourselves in
your hands. But you must not have the worse opinion of us
for our innocent frolic.

HEARTFREE.

Ladies, you may command our opinions in everything that
is to your advantage.   105

BELLINDA.

Then, sir, I command you to be of opinion that women are
sometimes better than they appear to be.

Lady Brute *and* Constant *talk apart.*

HEARTFREE.

Madam, you have made a convert of me in everything.
I'm grown a fool: I could be fond of a woman.

BELLINDA.

I thank you, sir, in the name of the whole sex.   110

HEARTFREE.

Which sex nothing but yourself could ever have atoned for.

BELLINDA.

Now has my vanity a devilish itch to know in what my merit
consists.

93. have] *Q1–3*; needs have *P.*

HEARTFREE.

In your humility, madam, that keeps you ignorant it consists
at all.   115

BELLINDA.

One other compliment with that serious face and I hate you
forever after.

HEARTFREE.

Some women love to be abused; is that it you would be at?

BELLINDA.

No, not that neither. But I'd have men talk plainly what's
fit for women to hear, without putting 'em either to a real, 120
or an affected blush.

HEARTFREE.

Why then, in as plain terms as I can find to express myself:
I could love you even to—matrimony itself a'most, egad.

BELLINDA.

Just as Sir John did her ladyship there. What think you?
Don't you believe one month's time might bring you down 125
to the same indifference, only clad in a little better manners
perhaps. Well, you men are unaccountable things, mad till
you have your mistresses, and then stark mad till you are rid
of 'em again. Tell me honestly, is not your patience put to a
much severer trial after possession than before?   130

HEARTFREE.

With a great many, I must confess, it is, to our eternal
scandal. But I—dear creature, do but try me.

BELLINDA.

That's the surest way indeed, to know, but not the safest.
—(*To* Lady Brute).   Madam, are not you for taking a turn
in the Great Walk? It's almost dark; nobody will know us. 135

LADY BRUTE.

Really I find myself something idle, Bellinda. Besides, I dote
upon this little odd private corner. But don't let my lazy
fancy confine you.

CONSTANT (*aside*).

So, she would be left alone with me, that's well.

BELLINDA.

Well, we'll take one turn and come to you again.   —(*To* 140
Heartfree.)   Come, sir, shall we go pry into the secrets of
the Garden? Who knows what discoveries we may make.

HEARTFREE.

Madam, I'm at your service.

CONSTANT (*to* Heartfree *aside*).

Don't make too much haste back, for, d'ye hear—I may be
busy.   145

HEARTFREE.

Enough.   *Exeunt* Bellinda *and* Heartfree.

LADY BRUTE.

Sure you think me scandalously free, Mr. Constant. I'm
afraid I shall lose your good opinion of me.

CONSTANT.

My good opinion, madam, is like your cruelty, never to be
removed.   150

LADY BRUTE.

But if I should remove my cruelty, then there's an end of
your good opinion.

CONSTANT.

There is not so strict an alliance between 'em neither. 'Tis
certain I should love you then better (if that be possible)
than I do now; and where I love, I always esteem.   155

LADY BRUTE.

Indeed, I doubt you much. Why, suppose you had a wife
and she should entertain a gallant.

CONSTANT.

If I gave her just cause, how could I justly condemn her?

LADY BRUTE.

Ah, but you'd differ widely about just causes.

CONSTANT.

But blows can bear no dispute.   160

LADY BRUTE.

Nor ill manners much, truly.

CONSTANT.

Then no woman upon earth has so just a cause as you have.

LADY BRUTE.

O, but a faithful wife is a beautiful character.

CONSTANT.

To a deserving husband, I confess it is.

LADY BRUTE.

But can his faults release my duty?   165

CONSTANT.

In equity, without doubt. And where laws dispense with
equity, equity should dispense with laws.

LADY BRUTE.

Pray let's leave this dispute, for you men have as much
witchcraft in your arguments as woman have in their eyes.

CONSTANT.

But whilst you attack me with your charms, 'tis but 170
reasonable I assault you with mine.

LADY BRUTE.

The case is not the same. What mischief we do, we can't help,
and therefore are to be forgiven.

CONSTANT.

Beauty soon obtains pardon, for the pain that it gives when it
applies the balm of compassion to the wound. But a fine 175
face and a hard heart is almost as bad as an ugly face and a
soft one; both very troublesome to many a poor gentleman.

LADY BRUTE.

Yes, and to many a poor gentlewoman, too I can assure you.
But pray which of 'em is it that most afflicts you?

CONSTANT.

Your glass and conscience will inform you, madam. But for 180
heaven's sake (for now I must be serious), if pity or if
gratitude can move you (*taking her hand*), if constancy and
truth have power to tempt you, if love, if adoration can
affect you, give me at least some hopes that time may do
what you perhaps mean never to perform; 'twill ease my 185
sufferings though not quench my flame.

LADY BRUTE.

Your sufferings eased, your flame would soon abate; and
that I would preserve, not quench it, sir.

CONSTANT.

Would you preserve it, nourish it with favors; for that's the
food it naturally requires. 190

LADY BRUTE.

Yet on that natural food, 'twould surfeit soon, should I
resolve to grant all that you would ask.

CONSTANT.

And in refusing all, you starve it. Forgive me therefore,

since my hunger rages, if I at last grow wild and in my
frenzy force at least this from you. (*Kissing her hand.*) Or 195
if you'd have my flame soar higher still, then grant me this,
and this, and this, and thousands more. (*Kissing first her
hand, then her neck.—Aside.*) For now's the time; she melts
into compassion.

LADY BRUTE (*aside*).

Poor coward virtue, how it shuns the battle. —O heavens! 200
let me go!

CONSTANT.

Aye, go, aye. Where shall we go, my charming angel? Into
this private arbor. Nay, let's lose no time. Moments are
precious.

LADY BRUTE.

And lovers wild. Pray let us stop here, at least for this time. 205

CONSTANT.

'Tis impossible. He that has power over you can have none
over himself.

LADY BRUTE.

Ah, I'm lost!

As he is forcing her into the arbor, Lady Fancyfull *and* Madamoiselle *bolt
out upon them and run over the stage.*

LADY FANCYFULL.

Fe, fe, fe, fe, fe.

MADAMOISELLE.

Fe, fe, fe, fe, fe. 210

CONSTANT.

Death and furies, who are these?

LADY BRUTE.

O heavens, I'm out of my wits; if they knew me, I'm
ruined.

CONSTANT.

Don't be frightened; ten thousand to one they are strangers
to you. 215

LADY BRUTE.

Whatever they are, I won't stay here a moment longer.

194. since] *Q1–3*; if since *P.*   194. if] *Q1–3*; *omit P.*

CONSTANT.

Whither will you go?

LADY BRUTE.

Home, as if the devil were in me. Lord, where's this
Bellinda now?

Enter Bellinda *and* Heartfree.

O, it's well you are come. I'm so frightened my hair stands 220
an end. Let's be gone, for heaven's sake.

BELLINDA.

Lord, what's the matter?

LADY BRUTE.

The devil's the matter; we are discovered. Here's a couple
of women have done the most impertinent thing. Away,
away, away, away, away! *Exit running.* [*The others follow.*] 225

Reenter Lady Fancyfull *and* Madamoiselle.

LADY FANCYFULL.

Well Madamoiselle, 'tis a prodigious thing how women
can suffer filthy fellows to grow so familiar with 'em.

MADAMOISELLE.

Ah matam, *il n'y a rien de si naturel.*

LADY FANCYFULL.

Fe, fe, fe. But O my heart! O jealousy, O torture, I'm upon
the rack. What shall I do? My lover's lost; I ne'er shall see 230
him mine. (*Pausing.*)   But I may be revenged, and that's
the same thing. Ah, sweet revenge! Thou welcome thought,
thou healing balsam to my wounded soul. Be but propitious
on this one occasion, I'll place my heaven in thee for all my
life to come.   235

To woman, how indulgent nature's kind.
No blast of fortune long disturbs her mind.
Compliance to her fate supports her still;
If love won't make her happy—mischief will.

Exeunt

---

228. *il . . . naturel*] there's nothing so natural.

ACT V

[V.i]   *Lady Fancyfull's house.*
                Enter Lady Fancyfull *and* Madamoiselle.

LADY FANCYFULL.
Well, Madamoiselle, did you dog the filthy things?
MADAMOISELLE.
O que oui, matam.
LADY FANCYFULL.
And where are they?
MADAMOISELLE.
Au logis.
LADY FANCYFULL.
What? Men and all?   5
MADAMOISELLE.
Tous ensemble.
LADY FANCYFULL.
O confidence! What, carry their fellows to their own
house?
MADAMOISELLE.
C'est que le mari n'y est pas.
LADY FANCYFULL.
No, so I believe, truly. But he shall be there, and quickly   10
too, if I can find him out. Well, 'tis a prodigious thing, to
see when men and women get together, how they fortify one
another in their impudence. But if that drunken fool, her
husband, be to be found in e'er a tavern in town, I'll send
him amongst 'em, I'll spoil their sport.   15
MADAMOISELLE.
En verité, matam, *çe serait dommage.*
LADY FANCYFULL.
'Tis in vain to oppose it, Madamoiselle; therefore never go
about it. For I am the steadiest creature in the world—
when I have determined to do mischief. So, come along. *Exeunt.*

---

2. *O que oui*] yes indeed.
4. *Au logis*] At home.
6. *Tous ensemble*] All together.
9. *C'est . . . pas*] It's because the husband's not there.
16. *En . . . dommage*] Truly, madam it would be a pity.

[V.ii]   *Sir John Brute's house.*
Enter Constant, Heartfree, Lady Brute, Bellinda *and* Lovewell.

LADY BRUTE.

But are you sure you don't mistake, Lovewell?

LOVEWELL.

Madam, I saw 'em all go into the tavern together, and my
master was so drunk he could scarce stand.   [*Exit.*]

LADY BRUTE.

Then, gentlemen, I believe we may venture to let you stay
and play at cards with us an hour or two; for they'll scarce   5
part till morning.

BELLINDA.

I think 'tis pity they should ever part.

CONSTANT.

The company that's here, madam.

LADY BRUTE.

Then, sir, the company that's here must remember to part
itself, in time.   10

CONSTANT.

Madam, we don't intend to forfeit your future favors by an
indiscreet usage of this. The moment you give us the signal,
we shan't fail to make our retreat.

LADY BRUTE.

Upon those conditions, then, let us sit down to cards.

Enter Lovewell.

[LOVEWELL.]

O Lord, madam, here's my master just staggering in upon   15
you. He has been quarrelsome yonder, and they have
kicked him out of the company.

LADY BRUTE.

Into the closet, gentlemen, for heaven's sake! I'll wheedle
him to bed if possible.   Constant *and* Heartfree *run into the closet.*

Enter Sir John, *all dirt and bloody.*

Ah, ah, he's all over blood!   20

SIR JOHN.

What the plague does the woman—squall for? Did you
never see a man in pickle before?

LADY BRUTE.

    Lord, where have you been?

SIR JOHN.

    I have been at—cuffs.

LADY BRUTE.

    I fear that is not all. I hope you are not wounded.   25

SIR JOHN.

    Sound as a roach, wife.

LADY BRUTE.

    I'm mighty glad to hear it.

SIR JOHN.

    You know, I think you lie.

LADY BRUTE.

    I know you do me wrong to think so, then. For heaven's my
witness, I had rather see my own blood trickle down than   30
yours.

SIR JOHN.

    Then will I be crucified.

LADY BRUTE.

    'Tis a hard fate, I should not be believed.

SIR JOHN.

    'Tis a damned atheistical age, wife.

LADY BRUTE.

    I am sure I have given you a thousand tender proofs, how   35
great my care is of you. Nay, spite of all your cruel thoughts
I'll still persist, and at this moment, if I can, persuade you
to lie down and sleep a little.

SIR JOHN.

    Why, do you think I am drunk, you slut, you?

LADY BRUTE.

    Heaven forbid I should! But I'm afraid you are feverish. Pray   40
let me feel your pulse.

SIR JOHN.

    Stand off and be damned.

LADY BRUTE.

    Why, I see your distemper in your very eyes. You are all
on fire. Pray go to bed, let me entreat you.

29. I know] *Q1–3*; *omit P.*   36. Nay] *Q1–3*; But *P.*
29. then] *Q1–3*; *omit P.*

SIR JOHN.

Come, kiss me then.   45

LADY BRUTE (*kissing him*).

There, now go. —(*Aside*.)   He stinks like poison.

SIR JOHN.

I see it goes damnably against your stomach. And therefore—
kiss me again.

LADY BRUTE.

Nay, now you fool me.

SIR JOHN.

Do't, I say.   50

LADY BRUTE (*aside*).

Ah Lord have mercy upon me.—Well, there. Now will you
go?

SIR JOHN.

Now wife, you shall see my gratitude. You give me two
kisses; I'll give you—two hundred.   *Kisses and tumbles her.*

LADY BRUTE.

O Lord! Pray, Sir John, be quiet. Heavens, what a pickle 55
am I in.

BELLINDA (*aside*).

If I were in her pickle, I'd call my gallant out of the closet,
and he should cudgel him soundly.

SIR JOHN.

So, now you being as dirty and as nasty as myself, we may
go pig together. But first I must have a cup of your cold tea, 60
wife.   *Going to the closet.*

LADY BRUTE [*aside*].

O, I'm ruined. —There's none there, my dear.

SIR JOHN.

I'll warrant you I'll find some, my dear.

LADY BRUTE.

You can't open the door; the lock's spoiled. I have been
turning and turning the key this half hour to no purpose. 65
I'll send for the smith tomorrow.

SIR JOHN.

There's ne'er a smith in Europe can open a door with more
expedition than I can do. As for example—pou! (*He*

50. Do't] *Q1–2, P*; Don't *Q3*.

---

bursts open the door with his foot.)   How now? What the devil
have we got here? Constant! Heartfree! And two whores   70
again, egad! This is the worst cold tea—that ever I met
with in my life.

Enter Constant *and* Heartfree.

LADY BRUTE *(aside).*

O Lord, what will become of us?

SIR JOHN.

Gentlemen, I am your very humble servant. I give you many
thanks. I see you take care of my family. I shall do all I can   75
to return the obligation.

CONSTANT.

Sir, how oddly soever this business may appear to you, you
would have no cause to be uneasy if you knew the truth of all
things. Your lady is the most virtuous woman in the world,
and nothing has passed but an innocent frolic.   80

HEARTFREE.

Nothing else, upon my honor, sir.

SIR JOHN.

You are both very civil gentlemen. And my wife there is a
very civil gentlewoman. Therefore I don't doubt but many
civil things have passed between you. Your very humble
servant.   85

LADY BRUTE *(aside to* Constant).

Pray be gone. He's so drunk he can't hurt us tonight, and
tomorrow morning you shall hear from us.

CONSTANT.

I'll obey you, madam. —Sir, when you are cool you'll
understand reason better. So then I shall take the pains to
inform you. If not, I wear a sword, sir, and so goodby to   90
you. Come along, Heartfree.   [*Exeunt* Constant *and* Heartfree.]

SIR JOHN.

Wear a sword, sir! And what of all that, sir? He comes to
my house, eats my meat, lies with my wife, dishonors my
family, gets a bastard to inherit my estate; and when I ask,
a civil account of all this—sir, says he, I wear a sword. Wear   95
a sword, sir? Yes sir, says he, I wear a sword. It may be a
good answer at cross purposes, but 'tis a damned one to
a man in my whimsical circumstance. Sir, says he, I wear a

sword. —(*To* Lady Brute.)   And what do you wear now
Ha, tell me. (*Sitting down in a great chair.*)   What? You 100
are modest and can't? Why then I'll tell you, you slut you.
You wear—an impudent lewd face—a damned designing
heart—and a tail full of———   *He falls fast asleep, snorin*

LADY BRUTE.

So, thanks to kind heaven, he's fast for some hours.

BELLINDA.

'Tis well he is so, that we may have time to lay our story 105
handsomely; for we must lie like the devil to bring ourselves off.

LADY BRUTE.

What shall we say Bellinda?

BELLINDA (*musing*).

I'll tell you. It must all light upon Heartfree and I. We'll
say he has courted me some time, but for reasons unknown 110
to us has ever been very earnest the thing might be kept from
Sir John. That therefore hearing him upon the stairs, he run
into the closet, though against our will, and Constant with
him, to prevent jealousy. And to give this a good impudent
face of truth (that I may deliver you from the trouble you 115
are in), I'll e'en (if he pleases) marry him.

LADY BRUTE.

I'm beholding to you, cousin, but that would be carrying
the jest a little too far for your own sake; you know he's a
younger brother and has nothing.

BELLINDA.

'Tis true; but I like him and have fortune enough to keep 120
above extremity. I can't say I would live with him in a cell
upon love and bread and butter; but I had rather have the
man I love, and a middle state of life, than that gentleman
in the chair there and twice your ladyship's splendor.

LADY BRUTE.

In truth, niece, you are in the right on't, for I am very 125
uneasy with my ambition. But perhaps, had I married as
you'll do, I might have been as ill used.

BELLINDA.

Some risk, I do confess, there always is. But if a man has
the least spark either of honor or good nature, he can never
use a woman ill that loves him and makes his fortune both. 130

Yet I must own to you, some little struggling I still have
with this teasing ambition of ours. For pride, you know, is as
natural to a woman as 'tis to a saint. I can't help being fond
of this rogue; and yet it goes to my heart to think I must
never whisk to Hyde Park with above a pair of horses, have 135
no coronet upon my coach nor a page to carry up my train.
But above all—that business of place—well, taking place
is a noble prerogative.

LADY BRUTE.

Especially after a quarrel.

BELLINDA.

Or of a rival. But pray say no more on't, for fear I change 140
my mind. For o' my conscience, were't not for your affair in
the balance, I should go near to pick up some odious man of
quality yet, and only take poor Heartfree for a gallant.

LADY BRUTE.

Then him you must have, however things go?

BELLINDA.

Yes.   145

LADY BRUTE.

Why we may pretend what we will, but 'tis a hard matter to
live without the man we love.

BELLINDA.

Especially when we are married to the man we hate. Pray
tell me, do the men of the town ever believe us virtuous
when they see us do so?   150

LADY BRUTE.

O, no; nor indeed hardly, let us do what we will. They most
of 'em think there is no such thing as virtue considered in
the strictest notions of it; and therefore when you hear 'em
say, such a one is a woman of reputation, they only mean
she's a woman of discretion. For they consider, we have no 155
more religion than they have, nor so much morality; and
between you and I, Bellinda, I'm afraid the want of inclination seldom protects any of us.

BELLINDA.

But what think you of the fear of being found out?

LADY BRUTE.

I think that never kept any woman virtuous long. We are not 160
such cowards neither. No, let us once pass fifteen, and we

have too good an opinion of our own cunning to believe the
world can penetrate into what we would keep a secret. And
so in short, we cannot reasonably blame the men for
judging of us by themselves.   165

BELLINDA.

But sure we are not so wicked as they are, after all.

LADY BRUTE.

We are as wicked, child, but our vice lies another way. Men
have more courage than we, so they commit more bold,
impudent sins. They quarrel, fight, swear, drink, blaspheme,
and the like. Whereas we, being cowards, only backbite, 170
tell lies, cheat at cards, and so forth. But 'tis late. Let's end
our discourse for tonight, and out of an excess of charity take
a small care of that nasty drunken thing there. Do but look
at him, Bellinda.

BELLINDA.

Ah, 'tis a savory dish.   175

LADY BRUTE.

As savory as 'tis, I'm cloyed with't. Prithee call the butler
to take away.

BELLINDA.

Call the butler? Call the scavenger. —(*To a servant
within*.) Who's there? Call Rasor. Let him take away his
master, scour him clean with a little soap and sand, and so 180
put him to bed.

LADY BRUTE.

Come Bellinda, I'll e'en lie with you tonight; and in the
morning we'll send for our gentlemen to set this matter even.

BELLINDA.

With all my heart.

LADY BRUTE (*making a low curtsy* [*to* Sir John]).

Good night, my dear.   185

BOTH.

Ha, ha, ha.   *Exeunt* [Lady Brute *and* Bellinda.]

Enter Rasor.

[RASOR].

My lady there's a wag. My master there's a cuckold.
Marriage is a slippery thing. Women have depraved
appetites. My lady's a wag. I have heard all, I have seen all,

I understand all, and I'll tell all; for my little Frenchwoman 190
loves news dearly. This story'll gain her heart or nothing
will. —(*To his master.*) Come, sir, your head's too full of
fumes at present to make room for your jealousy, but I
reckon we shall have rare work with you when your pate's
empty. Come; to your kennel, you cuckoldly drunken sot, 195
you.   *Carries him out upon his back.*

[V.iii]   *Lady Fancyfull's house.*
              Enter Lady Fancyfull *and* Madamoiselle.

LADY FANCYFULL.
But why did not you tell me before, Madamoiselle, that
Rasor and you were fond?
MADAMOISELLE.
De modesty hinder me, matam.
LADY FANCYFULL.
Why truly, modesty does often hinder us from doing things
we have an extravagant mind to. But does he love you well   5
enough yet, to do anything you bid him? Do you think to
oblige you he would speak scandal?
MADAMOISELLE.
Matam, to oblige your ladyship he shall speak blasphemy.
LADY FANCYFULL.
Why then, Madamoiselle, I'll tell you what you shall do.
You shall engage him to tell his master all that passed at   10
Spring Garden. I have a mind he should know what a wife
and a niece he has got.
MADAMOISELLE.
Il le fera, matam.

              Enter a Footman, *who speaks to* Madamoiselle *apart.*

FOOTMAN.
Madamoiselle, yonder's Mr. Rasor desires to speak with
you.   15
MADAMOISELLE.
Tell him, I come presently.   *Exit* Footman.
Rasor be dare, matam.

_____

13. *Il le fera*] He will.

LADY FANCYFULL.
That's fortunate. Well, I'll leave you together. And if you
find him stubborn, Madamoiselle—hark you—don't refuse
him a few little reasonable liberties to put him into humor.   20
MADAMOISLLE.
Laissez-moi faire.   *Exit* Lady Fancyfull.

Rasor peeps in, and seeing Lady Fancyfull *gone, runs to* Madamoiselle,
takes her about the neck and kisses her.

How now, confidence?
RASOR.
How now modesty?
MADAMOISELLE.
Who make you so familiar, sirrah?
RASOR.
My impudence, hussy.   25
MADAMOISELLE.
Stand off, rogue-face.
RASOR.
Ah, Madamoiselle, great news at our house.
MADAMOISELLE.
Wy wat be de matter?
RASOR.
The matter? Why, uptails-all's the matter.
MADAMOISELLE.
Tu te mocque de moi.   30
RASOR.
Now do you long to know the particulars—the time when,
the place where, the manner how. But I won't tell you a
word more.
MADAMOISELLE.
Nay, den dou kill me, Rasor.
RASOR.
Come, kiss me then.   *Clapping his hands behind him.* 35
MADAMOISELLE.
Nay, pridee tell me.

---

29. *uptails-all*] name of an old song, often used as here with sexual
suggestion.
30. *Tu . . . moi*] You're making fun of me.

RASOR (*going*).

    Goodbye to ye.

MADAMOISELLE.

    Hold, Hold! I will kiss dee.   *Kissing him.*

RASOR.

    So, that's civil. Why now, my pretty poll, my goldfinch, my
little waterwagtail. You must know that—come, kiss me   40
again.

MADAMOISELLE.

    I won't kiss dee no more.

RASOR.

    Goodbye to ye.

MADAMOISELLE.

    Doucement. Dare; *es tu content?*   *Kissing him.*

RASOR.

    So. Now I'll tell thee all. Why the news is, that cuckoldom   45
in folio is newly printed, and matrimony in quarto is just
going into the press. Will you buy any books, Madamoiselle?

MADAMOISELLE.

    Tu parle comme un libraire, de devil no understand dee.

RASOR.

    Why then, that I may make myself intelligible to a waiting-
woman, I'll speak like a *valet de chambre.* My lady has   50
cuckolded my master.

MADAMOISELLE.

    Bon.

RASOR.

    Which we take very ill from her hands, I can tell her that.
We can't yet prove matter of fact upon her.

MADAMOISELLE.

    N'importe.   55

RASOR.

    But we can prove that matter of fact had like to have been
upon her.

MADAMOISELLE.

    Oui da.

---

44. *Doucement . . . content*] Gently! There, are you content?
48. *Tu . . . libraire*] You talk like a bookseller.   52. *Bon*] Good.
55. *N'importe*] It doesn't matter.   58. *Oui da*] Yes indeed.

RASOR.

For we have such bloody circumstances—

MADAMOISELLE.

Sans doute.   60

RASOR.

That any man of parts may draw tickling conclusions from
'em.

MADAMOISELLE.

Fort bien.

RASOR.

We have found a couple of tight, well-built gentlemen
stuffed into her ladyship's closet.   65

MADAMOISELLE.

Le diable!

RASOR.

And I, in my particular person, have discovered a most
damnable plot how to persuade my poor master that all this
hide and seek, this will-in-the-wisp, has no other meaning
than a Christian marriage for sweet Mrs. Bellinda.   70

MADAMOISELLE.

Une mariage? Ah les drôlesses!

RASOR.

Don't you interrupt me, hussy; 'tis agreed, I say. And my
innocent lady, to wriggle herself out at the back door of the
business, turns marriage bawd to her niece and resolves to
deliver up her fair body to be tumbled and mumbled by that   75
young liquorish whipster, Heartfree. Now are you satisfied?

MADAMOISELLE.

No!

RASOR.

Right woman, always gaping for more.

MADAMOISELLE.

Dis be all den, dat dou know?

RASOR.

All? Aye, and a great deal, too, I think.   80

---

60. *Sans doute*] No doubt.
63. *Fort bien*] Very well.
66. *Le diable*] The devil.
71. *Une . . . drôlesses*] A marriage? O the scoundrels.

MADAMOISELLE.

Dou be fool, dou know noting. *Écoute, mon pauvre* Rasor.
Dou see des two eyes? Des two eyes have see de devil.

RASOR.

The woman's mad.

MADAMOISELLE.

In Spring Garden, dat rogue Constant meet dy lady.

RASOR.

Bon.   85

MADAMOISELLE.

I'll tell dee no more.

RASOR.

Nay, prithee, my swan.

MADAMOISELLE.

Come, kiss me den.

Clapping her hands behind her, as he had done before.

RASOR.

I won't kiss you, not I.

MADAMOISELLE.

Adieu.   90

RASOR.

Hold! Now proceed.   *Gives her a hearty kiss.*

MADAMOISELLE.

À ça. I hide myself in one cunning place where I hear all and
see all. First dy drunken master come *mal à propos.* But de sot
no know his own dear wife, so he leave her to her sport.
Den de game begin.   95

As she speaks, Rasor *still acts the man and she the woman.*

De lover say soft ting.
De lady look upon de ground.
He take her by de hand.
She turn her head, one oder way.
Den he squeeze very hard.   100
Den she pull—very softly.
Den he take her in his arm.

99. one] *Q1*; on *Q2–3, P.*

---

81. *Écoute . . . Rasor*] Listen, my poor Rasor.
92. *À ça*] Well now.
93. *mal à propos*] at the wrong time.

Den she give him leetel pat.
Den he kiss her tetons.
Den she say, pish, nay, see.   105
Den he tremble.
Den she—sigh.
Den he pull her into de arbor.
Den she pinch him.

RASOR.

Aye, but not so hard, you baggage you.   110

MADAMOISELLE.

Den he grow bold.
She grow weak.
He tro her down.
Il tombe dessus.
Le diable assiste,   115
Il emporte tout.

    Rasor struggles with her as if he would throw her down.

Stand off, sirrah!

RASOR.

You have set me afire, you jade you.

MADAMOISELLE.

Den go to de river and quench dyself.

RASOR.

What an unnatural harlot 'tis.   120

MADAMOISELLE *(looking languishingly on him).*

Rasor.

RASOR.

Madamoiselle.

MADAMOISELLE.

Dou no love me?

RASOR.

Not love thee! More than a Frenchman does soup.

MADAMOISELLE.

Den dou will refuse noting dat I bid dee?   125

RASOR.

Don't bid me be damned then.

123. me?] *P*; me. *Q 1–3.*

___

104. *tetons*] breasts.
114–116. *Il . . . tout*] He falls on top; the devil helps, he carries it all
away.

MADAMOISELLE.

No, only tell dy master all I have tell dee of dy laty.

RASOR.

Why, you little malicious strumpet, you; should you like to be served so?

MADAMOISELLE.

Dou dispute den? Adieu.   130

RASOR.

Hold. But why wilt thou make me be such a rogue, my dear?

MADAMOISELLE.

Voilà un vrai Anglais: il est amoureux et cependent il veut raisonner. Va-t-en au diable!

RASOR.

Hold once more. In hopes thou'lt give me up thy body, I 135 resign thee up my soul.

MADAMOISELLE.

Bon. Écoute donc: if dou fail me, I never see dee more; if dou obey me, *je m'abandonne à toi.*

She takes him about the neck and gives him a smacking kiss. Exit Madamoiselle.

RASOR (*licking his lips*).

Not be a rogue! *Amor vincit omnia.*   *Exit* Rasor.

Enter Lady Fancyfull *and* Madamoiselle.

LADY FANCYFULL.

Marry, say ye? Will the two things marry?   140

MADAMOISELLE.

On le va faire, matam.

LADY FANCYFULL.

Look you, Madamoiselle, in short, I can't bear it—no, I find I can't. If once I see 'em a-bed together, I shall have ten thousand thoughts in my head will make me run distracted. Therefore run and call Rasor back immediately, for some- 145

133–134. *Voilà . . . diable*] Here's a true Englishman; he's in love and still he wants to reason. Go to the devil.

137. *Bon. Écoute donc*] Good. So listen.

138. *je . . . toi*] I'll surrender myself to you.

141. *On le va faire*] It's going to happen.

thing must be done to stop this impertinent wedding. If I can but defer it four and twenty hours, I'll make such work about town with that little pert slut's reputation, he shall as soon marry a witch.

MADAMOISELLE (*aside*).

La voilà bien intentionée.   *Exeunt.*   150

[V.iv]   *Constant's lodgings.*
Enter Constant *and* Heartfree.

CONSTANT.

But what dost think will come of this business?

HEARTFREE.

'Tis easier to think what will not come on't.

CONSTANT.

What's that?

HEARTFREE.

A challenge. I know the knight too well for that. His dear body will always prevail upon his noble soul to be quiet.   5

CONSTANT.

But though he dare not challenge me, perhaps he may venture to challenge his wife.

HEARTFREE.

Not if you whisper him in the ear, you won't have him do't; and there's no other way left that I see. For as drunk as he was, he'll remember you and I were where we should not   10 be, and I don't think him quite blockhead enough yet to be persuaded we were got into his wife's closet only to peep in her prayer book.

Enter Servant *with a letter.*

SERVANT.

Sir here's a letter; a porter brought it.   [*Exit*].

CONSTANT.

O ho, here's instructions for us. —(*Reads.*) "The accident   15 that has happened has touched our invention to the quick. We would fain come off without your help, but find that's

147. but defer it] *Q1–2*; defer it but *Q3, P.*

_____

150. *La . . . intentionée*] There she's well-meaning.

– 103 –

impossible. In a word, the whole business must be thrown upon a matrimonial intrigue between your friend and mine. But if the parties are not fond enough to go quite through with the matter, 'tis sufficient for our turn, they own the the design. We'll find pretenses enough to break the match. Adieu." —Well, woman for invention. How long would my blockhead have been a-producing this. Hey, Heartfree! What, musing, man? Prithee be cheerful. What sayst thou, friend, to this matrimonial remedy? 20

25

HEARTFREE.

Why, I say it's worse than the disease.

CONSTANT.

Here's a fellow for you. There's beauty and money on her side, and love up to the ears on his; and yet—

HEARTFREE.

And yet, I think, I may reasonably be allowed to boggle at marrying the niece in the very moment that you are a-debauching the aunt. 30

CONSTANT.

Why truly, there may be something in that. But have not you a good opinion enough of your own parts to believe you could keep a wife to yourself? 35

HEARTFREE.

I should have, if I had a good opinion enough of hers to believe she could do as much by me. For to do 'em right, after all, the wife seldom rambles till the husband shows her the way.

CONSTANT.

'Tis true; a man of real worth scarce ever is a cuckold but by his own fault. Women are not naturally lewd; there must be something to urge 'em to it. They'll cuckold a churl out of revenge, a fool because they despise him, a beast because they loathe him. But when they make bold with a man they once had a well-grounded value for, 'tis because they first see themselves neglected by him. 40

45

HEARTFREE.

Nay, were I well assured that I should never grow Sir John,

31-32. a-debauching] *Q1–3*; de-
bauching *P*.

I ne'er should fear Bellinda'd play my lady. But our weakness, thou knowest, my friend, consists in that very change we so impudently throw upon (indeed) a steadier and more   50
generous sex.

CONSTANT.

Why, faith, we are a little impudent in that matter, that's the truth on't. But this is wonderful, to see you grown so warm an advocate for those (but t'other day) you took so much pains to abuse.   55

HEARTFREE.

All revolutions run into extremes: the bigot makes the boldest athiest, and the coyest saint the most extravagant strumpet. But prithee advise me in this good and evil, this life and death, this blessing and cursing that is set before me. Shall I marry—or die a maid?   60

CONSTANT.

Why faith, Heartfree, matrimony is like an army going to engage. Love's the forlorn hope, which is soon cut off; the marriage knot is the main body, which may stand buff a long, long time; and repentance is the rear guard, which rarely gives ground as long as the main battle has a being.   65

HEARTFREE.

Conclusion then: you advise me to whore on, as you do.

CONSTANT.

That's not concluded yet. For though marriage be a lottery in which there are a wondrous many blanks, yet there is one inestimable lot in which the only heaven on earth is written. Would your kind fate but guide your hand to that, though I   70
were wrapped in all that luxury itself could clothe me with, I still should envy you.

HEARTFREE.

And justly too; for to be capable of loving one, doubtless is better than to possess a thousand. But how far that capacity's in me, alas I know not.   75

CONSTANT.

But you would know?

HEARTFREE.

I would so.

---

63. *stand buff*] stand firm.

CONSTANT.

Matrimony will inform you. Come, one flight of resolution
carries you to the land of experience, where in a very
moderate time you'll know the capacity of your soul and   80
your body both, or I'm mistaken.   *Exeunt.*

[V.v]   *Sir John Brute's house.*
              Enter Lady Brute *and* Bellinda.

BELLINDA.

Well, madam, what answer have you from 'em?

LADY BRUTE.

That they'll be here this moment. I fancy 'twill end in a
wedding. I'm sure he's a fool if it don't. Ten thousand
pound, and such a lass as you are, is no contemptible offer
to a younger brother. But are not you under strange agita-   5
tions? Prithee how does your pulse beat?

BELLINDA.

High and low, I have much ado to be valiant; sure it must
feel very strange to go to bed to a man.

LADY BRUTE.

Um, it does feel a little odd at first, but it will soon grow
easy to you.   10

              Enter Constant *and* Heartfree.

Good morrow, gentlemen. How have you slept after your
adventure?

HEARTFREE.

Some careful thoughts, ladies, on your accounts have kept
us waking.

BELLINDA.

And some careful thoughts on your own, I believe, have   15
hindered you from sleeping. Pray how does this matrimonial
project relish with you?

HEARTFREE.

Why faith, e'en as storming towns does with soldiers, where
the hopes of delicious plunder banishes the fear of being
knocked on the head.   20

7. sure it must] *P; omit Q1–3.*

—106—

BELLINDA.

Is it then possible, after all, that you dare think of downright
lawful wedlock?

HEARTFREE.

Madam, you have made me so foolhardy I dare do anything.

BELLINDA.

Then sir, I challenge you, and matrimony's the spot where
I expect you.   25

HEARTFREE.

'Tis enough; I'll not fail. —(*Aside.*)   So, now I am in for
Hobs's voyage, a great leap in the dark.

LADY BRUTE.

Well, gentlemen, this matter being concluded then, have
you got your lessons ready? For Sir John is grown such an
atheist of late, he'll believe nothing upon easy terms.   30

CONSTANT.

We'll find ways to extend his faith, madam. But pray, how
do you find him this morning?

LADY BRUTE.

Most lamentably morose, chewing the cud after last night's
discovery, of which however he had but a confused notion
e'en now. But I'm afraid his *valet de chambre* has told him all,   35
for they are very busy together at this moment. When I
told him of Bellinda's marriage, I had no other answer but a
grunt; from which you may draw what conclusions you
think fit. But to your notes, gentlemen, he's here.

Enter Sir John *and* Rasor.

CONSTANT.

Good morrow, sir.   40

HEARTFREE.

Good morrow, Sir John. I'm very sorry my indescretion
should cause so much disorder in your family.

---

27. Hobs's] *Q1–2*; Hob's *Q3*;   35. his] *Q1*; the *Q2–3*, *P*.
Hobbes's *P*.

---

27. *Hob's voyage*] perhaps topical. Attempts to connect the phrase with
the Hobson of Hobson's choice or Thomas Hobbes (see reading of P) are
unconvincing.

SIR JOHN.

Disorders generally come from indiscretions, sir, 'tis no
strange thing at all.

LADY BRUTE.

I hope, my dear, you are satisfied there was no wrong   45
intended you.

SIR JOHN.

None, my dove.

BELLINDA.

If not, I hope my consent to marry Mr. Heartfree will convince you. For as little as I know of amours, sir, I can assure
you, one intrigue is enough to bring four people together   50
without further mischief.

SIR JOHN.

And I know too, that intrigues tend to procreation of more
kinds than one. One intrigue will beget another as soon as
beget a son or a daughter.

CONSTANT.

I am very sorry, sir, to see you still seem unsatisfied with a   55
lady whose more than common virtue, I am sure, were she
my wife, should meet a better usage.

SIR JOHN.

Sir, if her conduct has put a trick upon her virtue, her
virtue's the bubble, but her husband's the loser.

CONSTANT.

Sir, you have received a sufficient answer already to justify   60
both her conduct and mine. You'll pardon me for meddling
in your family affairs, but I perceive I am the man you are
jealous of, and therefore it concerns me.

SIR JOHN.

Would it did not concern me, and then I should not care who
it concerned.   65

CONSTANT.

Well, sir, if truth and reason won't content you, I know but
one way more which, if you think fit, you may take.

SIR JOHN.

Lord, sir, you are very hasty; if I had been found at prayers

43. S.P. SIR JOHN] *ed. of 1776*;   52. tend] *Q2–3, P*; tends *Q1*.
Constant *Q1–3, P*.

in your wife's closet, I should have allowed you twice as
much time to come to yourself in.   70

CONSTANT.

Nay, sir, if time be all you want, we have no quarrel.

HEARTFREE.

I told you how the sword would work upon him.

                                            Sir John *muses*.

CONSTANT.

Let him muse; however, I'll lay fifty pound our foreman
brings us in, not guilty.

SIR JOHN (*aside*).

'Tis well, 'tis very well. In spite of that young jade's matri-   75
monial intrigue, I am a downright stinking cuckold.   (*Putting his hand to his forehead.*)   Here they are—boo! Methinks
I could butt with a bull. What the plague did I marry her
for? I knew she did not like me; if she had, she would have
lain with me, for I would have done so because I liked her.   80
But that's past and I have her. And now, what shall I do
with her? If I put my horns in my pocket, she'll grow
insolent. If I don't, that goat there, that stallion, is ready to
whip me through the guts. The debate then is reduced to
this, shall I die a hero or live a rascal? Why, wiser men than   85
I have long since concluded that a living dog is better than
a dead lion.   —(*To* Constant *and* Heartfree.)   Gentlemen,
now my wine and my passion are governable, I must own,
I have never observed anything in my wife's course of life to
back me in my jealousy of her. But jealousy's a mark of love;   90
so she need not trouble her head about it, as long as I make
no more words on't.

Lady Fancyfull *enters disguised and addresses to* Bellinda *apart*.

CONSTANT.

I am glad to see your reason rule at last. Give me your hand;
I hope you'll look upon me as you are wont.

SIR JOHN.

Your humble servant.   —(*Aside.*)   A wheedling son of a   95
whore.

82. in] *Q1–3*; into *P*.

HEARTFREE.

And that I may be sure you are friends with me too, pray
give me your consent to wed your niece.

SIR JOHN.

Sir, you have it with all my heart, damn me if you han't.
—(*Aside.*) 'Tis time to get rid of her: a young, pert pimp, 100
she'll make an incomparable bawd in a little time.

Enter a servant, who gives Heartfree *a letter.*

BELLINDA.

Heartfree your husband, say you? 'Tis impossible.

LADY FANCYFULL.

Would to kind heaven it were; but 'tis too true, and in the
world there lives not such a wretch. I'm young, and either I
have been flattered by my friends as well as glass, or nature 105
has been kind and generous to me. I had a fortune too, was
greater far than he could ever hope for. But with my heart,
I am robbed of all the rest. I'm slighted and I'm beggared
both at once. I have scarce a bare subsistence from the
villain, yet dare complain to none, for he has sworn if e'er 110
'tis known I am his wife, he'll murder me.   *Weeping.*

BELLINDA.

The traitor.

LADY FANCYFULL.

I accidentally was told he courted you. Charity soon pre-
vailed upon me to prevent your misery. And, as you see,
I'm still so generous even to him as not to suffer he should 115
do a thing for which the law might take away his life.

Weeping.

BELLINDA.

Poor creature, how I pity her!   *They continue talking aside.*

HEARTFREE (*aside*).

Death and damnation! Let me read it again. —(*Reads.*)
"Though I have a particular reason not to let you know who
I am till I see you, yet you'll easily believe 'tis a faithful 120
friend that gives you this advice. I have lain with Bellinda."
(Good.) "I have a child by her"—(better and better)—
"which is now at nurse"—(heaven be praised)—"and I

---

116. *law ... life*] Bigamy could be punished by death until 1828.

think the foundation laid for another." (Ha! Old trupenny!)
"No rack could have tortured this story from me, but 125
friendship has done it. I heard of your design to marry her
and could not see you abused. Make use of my advice, but
keep my secret till I ask you for't again. Adieu."

Exit Lady Fancyfull.

CONSTANT (*to* Bellinda).

Come madam, shall we send for the parson? I doubt here's
no business for the lawyer; younger brothers have nothing 130
to settle but their hearts, and that I believe my friend here
has already done, very faithfully.

BELLINDA (*scornfully*).

Are you sure, sir, there are no old mortgages upon it?

HEARTFREE (*coldly*).

If you think there are, madam, it mayn't be amiss to defer
the marriage till you are sure they are paid off.   135

BELLINDA (*aside*).

How the galled horse kicks! —(*To* Heartfree.) We'll
defer it as long as you please, sir.

HEARTFREE.

The more time we take to consider on't, madam, the less
apt we shall be to commit oversights. Therefore, if you
please, we'll put it off for just nine months.   140

BELLINDA.

Guilty consciences make men cowards. I don't wonder you
want time to resolve.

HEARTFREE.

And they make women desperate. I don't wonder you were
so quickly determined.

BELLINDA.

What does the fellow mean?   145

HEARTFREE.

What does the lady mean?

SIR JOHN.

Zounds, what do you both mean?

Heartfree *and* Bellinda *walk chafing about.*

---

124. *old trupenny*] trusty fellow. The association of the term with the Ghost
in *Hamlet* is so strong that Heartfree's thought probably is, "Canst work i'
th' earth so fast? O worthy pioneer" (*Hamlet*, I.v.171).

RASOR (*aside*).

Here is so much sport going to be spoiled, it makes me ready
to weep again. A pox o'this impertinent Lady Fancyfull and
her plots and her French woman too. She's a whimsical, 150
ill-natured bitch, and when I have got my bones broke in
her service, 'tis ten to one but my recompense is a clap.
I hear 'em tittering without still. Icod, I'll e'en go lug 'em
both in by the ears and discover the plot, to secure my
pardon.   *Exit* Rasor. 155

CONSTANT.

Prithee explain, Heartfree.

HEARTFREE.

A fair deliverance, thank my stars and my friend.

BELLINDA.

'Tis well it went no farther. A base fellow.

LADY BRUTE.

What can be the meaning of all this?

BELLINDA.

What's his meaning, I don't know. But mine is, that if I had 160
married him—I had had no husband.

HEARTFREE.

And what's her meaning, I don't know. But mine is, that if
I had married her—I had had wife enough.

SIR JOHN.

Your people of wit have got such cramp ways of expressing
themselves, they seldom comprehend one another. Pox take 165
you both, will you speak that you may be understood?

Enter Rasor *in sackcloth, pulling in* Lady Fancyfull *and* Madamoiselle.

RASOR.

If they won't, here comes an interpreter.

LADY BRUTE.

Heavens, what have we here?

RASOR.

A villain, but a repenting villain. Stuff which saints in all
ages have been made of.   170

ALL.

Rasor!

LADY BRUTE.

What means this sudden metamorphose?

RASOR.

Nothing, without my pardon.

LADY BRUTE.

What pardon do you want?

RASOR.

Imprimis, your ladyship's, for a damnable lie made upon 175
your spotless virtue and set to the tune of Spring Garden.
—(*To* Sir John.)   Next, at my generous master's feet I bend,
for interrupting his more noble thoughts with phantoms of
disgraceful cuckoldom.   —(*To* Constant.)   Thirdly, I to
this gentleman apply, for making him the hero of my 180
romance.   —(*To* Heartfree.)   Fourthly, your pardon,
noble sir, I ask, for clandestinely marrying you without
either bidding of banns, bishop's license, friends' consent—
or your own knowledge.   —(*To* Bellinda.)   And lastly, to
my good young lady's clemency I come, for pretending the 185
corn was sowed in the ground before ever the plough had
been in the field.

SIR JOHN (*aside*).

So that after all, 'tis a moot point whether I am a cuckold
or not.

BELLINDA.

Well sir, upon condition you confess all, I'll pardon you 190
myself, and try to obtain as much from the rest of the company. But I must know then, who 'tis has put you upon all
this mischief.

RASOR.

Satan and his equipage. Woman tempted me, lust weakened
me, and so the devil overcame me; as fell Adam, so fell I. 195

BELLINDA.

Then pray, Mr. Adam, will you make us acquainted with
your Eve?

RASOR (*to* Madamoiselle).

Unmask, for the honor of France.

ALL.

Madamoiselle!

MADAMOISELLE.

Me ask ten tousand pardon of all de good company.   200

SIR JOHN.

Why, this mystery thickens instead of clearing up.   —(*To*

Rasor.)   You son of a whore you, put us out of our pain.

RASOR.

One moment brings sunshine. (*Showing* Madamoiselle.)
'Tis true, this is the woman that tempted me. But this is the
serpent that tempted the woman. And if my prayers might 205
be heard, her punishment for so doing should be like the
serpent's of old. (*Pulls off Lady Fancyfull's mask.*) She
should lie upon her face all the days of her life.

ALL.

Lady Fancyfull!

BELLINDA.

Impertinent.   210

LADY BRUTE.

Ridiculous.

ALL.

Ha, ha, ha, ha, ha.

BELLINDA.

I hope your ladyship will give me leave to wish you joy,
since you have owned your marriage yourself. Mr. Heartfree, I vow 'twas strangely wicked in you to think of another 215
wife when you had one already so charming as her ladyship.

ALL.

Ha, ha, ha, ha, ha.

LADY FANCYFULL (*aside*).

Confusion seize 'em as it seizes me.

MADAMOISELLE.

Que le diable étouffe çe maraud de Rasor.

BELLINDA.

Your ladyship seems disordered; a breeding qualm, per- 220
haps. Mr. Heartfree, your bottle of Hungary Water to your
lady. Why madam, he stands as unconcerned as if he were
your husband in earnest.

LADY FANCYFULL.

Your mirth's as nauseous as yourself, Bellinda. You think

219. *étouffe*] *ed. of 1776*; e toute   221. Hungary] *P*; Hungry *Q1–3*.
Q1–3, P.

---

219. *Que . . . Rasor*] May the devil choke that scoundrel Rasor.
221. *Hungary water*] a preparation of rosemary flowers infused in wine, to
relieve qualms or fainting spells; first made for a queen of Hungary.

you triumph o'er a rival now. *Hélas ma pauvre fille.* Where'er 225
I'm rival there's no cause for mirth. No, my poor wretch,
'tis from another principle I have acted. I knew that thing
there would make so perverse a husband, and you so impertinent a wife, that lest your mutual plagues should make
you both run mad, I charitably would have broke the 230
match. He, he, he, he, he.

> *Exit laughing affectedly,* Madamoiselle *following her.*

MADAMOISELLE.

He, he, he, he, he.

ALL.

Ha, ha, ha, ha, ha.

SIR JOHN (*aside*).

Why now this woman will be married to somebody too.

BELLINDA.

Poor creature, what a passion she's in. But I forgive her.   235

HEARTFREE.

Since you have so much goodness for her, I hope you'll
pardon my offense too, madam.

BELLINDA.

There will be no great difficulty in that, since I am guilty of
an equal fault.

HEARTFREE.

Then pardons being passed on all sides, pray let's to church 240
to conclude the day's work.

CONSTANT.

But before you go, let me treat you pray with a song a new-
married lady made within this week; it may be of use to you
both.

SONG

1.

When yielding first to Damon's flame,   245
   I sunk into his arms,
He swore he'd ever be the same,
   Then rifled all my charms.

---

225. o'er] *Q 1–3*; over *P.*

---

225. *Hélas . . . fille*] Alas my poor daughter.

But fond of what h'ad long desired,
    Too greedy of his prey,   250
My shepherd's flame, alas, expired
    Before the verge of day.

                        2.

My innocence in lovers' wars
    Reproached his quick defeat.
Confused, ashamed, and bathed in tears,   255
    I mourned his cold retreat.
At length, ah shepherdess, cried he,
    Would you my fire renew,
Alas you must retreat like me,
    I'm lost if you pursue.   260

HEARTFREE.

So madam, now had the parson but done his business—

BELLINDA.

You'd be half weary of your bargain.

HEARTFREE.

No sure, I might dispense with one night's lodging.

BELLINDA.

I'm ready to try, sir.

HEARTFREE.

Then let's to church.   265
            And if it be our chance to disagree—

BELLINDA.

            Take heed: the surly husband's fate you see.

                        FINIS

249. h'ad] *Q1–3*, *P*; he'd *ed. of
1776.*

_____

  263. *dispense with*] agree to.

EPILOGUE

By another hand
Spoken by Lady Brute and Bellinda

LADY BRUTE.	No epilogue?
BELLINDA.	I swear I know of none.
LADY BRUTE.	Lord! How shall we excuse it to the town?
BELLINDA.	Why, we must e'en say something of our own.
LADY BRUTE.	Our own! Aye, that must needs be precious stuff.
BELLINDA.	I'll lay my life they'll like it well enough. 5
	Come, faith, begin.
LADY BRUTE.	Excuse me, after you.
BELLINDA.	Nay, pardon me for that, I know my cue.
LADY BRUTE.	O for the world I would not have precedence.
BELLINDA.	O lord!
LADY BRUTE.	I swear—
BELLINDA.	O fie!
LADY BRUTE.	I'm all obedience.
	First then, know all, before our doom is fixed, 10
	The third day is for us—
BELLINDA.	Nay, and the sixt.
LADY BRUTE.	We speak not from the poet now, nor is it
	His cause—(I want a rhyme)—
BELLINDA.	That we solicit.
LADY BRUTE.	Then sure you cannot have the hearts to be severe
	And damn us—
BELLINDA.	Damn us! Let 'em if they dare. 15
LADY BRUTE.	Why, if they should, what punishment remains?
BELLINDA.	Eternal exile from behind our scenes.
LADY BRUTE.	But if they're kind, that sentence we'll recall.
	We can be grateful—
BELLINDA.	And have wherewithall.

11. sixt] *Q1*; sixth *Q2–3, P*.

---

11. *third day*] The third performance (with the sixth and ninth) of a play was the author's benefit. Vanbrugh is perhaps tactfully stating that he is giving up his profit to the actors.

17. *exile . . . scenes*] It was not unusual for members of the audience to be visiting backstage even during the performance.

LADY BRUTE.   But at grand treaties, hope not to be trusted   20
               Before preliminaries are adjusted.
BELLINDA.   You know the time, and we appoint this place
               Where, if you please, we'll meet and sign the peace.

---

23. *sign the peace*] another reference to the hoped-for peace that was not to come until September, 1697.

Appendix A

Two Songs

1

This song illustrates one aspect of the stage history of the play, the addition of new songs. Since Colonel Bully has almost no lines, his became an obvious part for a singer. There is no entirely logical place for this song, but after IV.i or before or after IV.iii would do easily. The song clearly refers to Sir John in his parson's disguise, and this raises problems about the revision of the play, to be discussed in Appendix B.[1]

The text is taken from *The Musical Miscellany, being a Collection of Choice Songs Set to the Violin and Flute, by the Most Eminent Masters* (London, 1729), I. 66–68; there probably was no other printing.

Tippling John
Sung by Mr. Harper, in The Provoked Wife

As tippling John was jogging on,
    Upon the riot night,
With tottering pace and fiery face,
    Suspicious of high flight,
The guards who took him, by his look
    For some chief firebrand,
Asked whence he came, what was his name;
    Who are you? Stand, friend, stand.

I'm going home, from meeting come;
    Aye, says one, that's the case:
Some meeting he has burnt, you see,
    The flame's still in his face.

---

1 The most recent discussion of the problem is by Frank M. Patterson in *English Language Notes*, IV (1966), 19–23. Both Professor Patterson and I owe our knowledge of the song to the late Professor Charles B. Woods.

John thought 'twas time to purge the crime,
    And said, 'twas his intent
For to assuage his thirsty rage;
    That meeting 'twas he meant.

Come friend, be plain, you trifle in vain,
    Says one, pray let us know,
That we may find how you're inclined,
    Are you high church or low?

John said to that, I'll tell you what,
    To end debates and strife,
All I can say, this is the way
    I steer my course of life.

I ne'er to Bow nor Burgess go,
    To steeple-house nor hall;
The brisk bar bell best suits my zeal,
    With, "Gentlemen, d'ye call?"

Now judge, am I low church or high,
    From tavern or the steeple,
Whose merry toll exalts the soul
    And makes us high-flown people.

The guards came on and looked at John
    With countenance most pleasant.
By whisper round they all soon found
    He was no dangerous peasant;
So while John stood the best he could,
    Expecting their decision,
Pox on't, says one, let him be gone,
    He's of our own religion.

2

It is hard to believe that the following rather sad piece of gaiety was written for *The Provoked Wife*, or even that all the stanzas belong together. It first appears in the 1776 edition of the play (from which it is here reprinted), just after the song in III.ii, with the statement: "Instead of this song by Lord Rake, the following by Colonel Bully is now sung at the theatre." In an undated broadside near the end of the eighteenth century it is called "A Scotch Medley introduced in The Provoked Wife," and it is substituted for Lord Rake's song (usually with the second stanza omitted) in play collections such as Bell's and Mrs. Inchbald's. A further testimony to the song's popularity comes from Garrick's final performance as Sir John on April 30, 1776. "When the Song Encor'd Mr Garrick said Come Col. give us that Song again for two very good Reasons, the first because your friends desire it—and Secondly because I believe I shall never be in such good company again".[2]

Sung by Col. Bully

I.

We're gayly yet, and we're gayly yet,
And we's not very fow, but we're gayly yet.
Then sit ye a while, and tipple a bit,
For we's not very fow, but we're gayly yet.

II.

There was a lad, and they cau'd him Dicky,
He ga' me a kiss, and I bit his lippy.
Then under my apron he showed me a trick;
And we's not very fow, but we're gayly yet.
      And we're gayly yet, etc., etc.

III.

There were three lads and they were clad,
There were three lasses and them they had.
Three trees in the orchard are newly sprung,
And we's a' git geer enough, we're but young.
      And we're gayly yet, etc., etc.

IV.

Then up went Ailey, Ailey, up went Ailey now;
Then up went Ailey, quo Crumma, we's got a
      roaring fow.
And one was kissed in the barn, another was
      kissed on the green,
And t'other behind the pease-stack, till the mow
      flew up to her eyen.
      Then up went Ailey, Ailey, etc., etc.

2 *The London Stage*, Part IV, ed. George Winchester Stone (Carbondale, Ill., 1962), pp. 1972–1973.

V.

Now fie, John Thompson, run
Gin ever ye run in your life;
De'el get ye, but hye, my dear Jack,
There's a mon got to bed with your wife.
    Then up went Ailey, etc., etc.

VI.

Then away John Thompson ran,
And egad he ran with speed,
But before he had run his length,
The false loon had done the deed.
    Then up went Ailey, etc., etc.

Appendix B

The Revised Scenes

These altered scenes were first published in a Dublin edition of 1743 which notes on its title page, "In which is inserted an original scene, never before printed."[1] They next appear in Vanbrugh's *Plays* (London, 1759), I, 208 ff., as an appendix to the play, with the explanation, "Upon the Revival of this Play in 1725, Sir *John Vanbrugh* thought proper to write the two following Scenes, in the room of those printed . . . ." Further information in the preface to this edition is derived entirely from Colley Cibber—material to be discussed in a moment. Later London editions, from 1765 on, simply substitute these new scenes. One later line, Sir John's "Why, I have been beating the watch and scandalizing the clergy," (IV.iv.54) refers to this escapade, and it was not until 1776 that the printed texts changed "the clergy" to "the women of quality" to make all consistent again. The popularity of the scenes is perhaps suggested by frontispiece illustrations in late eighteenth- and nineteenth-century collections, where Sir John in woman's attire is the usual subject; the Bell edition of 1780 with Garrick in this costume shows the scene at its best.

There is some disagreement about both date and authorship of this material, but with our present knowledge of the stage history of the play we can state, with practical certainty, that it was prepared for the 1726 production at Drury Lane. To be sure, the play was announced "with alterations" for its revival in 1706, on which basis Genest and many later scholars assumed that the change in Sir John's disguise was made then, presumably in deference to Jeremy Collier's views. But against this is Colley Cibber's statement:

In 1725 we were call'd upon, in a manner that could not be resisted, to revive the *Provok'd Wife*, a Comedy which, while we

[1] There were apparently two issues, one printed by S. Powell for George Rick, the other by Edw. Bate for James Kelburn.

– 123 –

found our Account in keeping the Stage clear of those loose Liberties it had formerly too justly been charg'd with, we had laid aside for some Years. The Author, Sir *John Vanbrugh*, who was conscious of what it had too much of, was prevail'd upon to substitute a new-written Scene in the Place of one in the fourth Act, where the Wantonness of his Wit and Humour had (originally) made a Rake talk like a Rake in the borrow'd Habit of a Clergyman: To avoid which Offence, he clapt the same Debauchee into the Undress of a Woman of Quality.[2]

The production was staged on January 11, 1726—still in Vanbrugh's lifetime—and the often-repeated advertisement, "Revised by the author," clearly supports Cibber. There are minor inaccuracies in his statement. The play had not exactly been "laid aside for some years," but was intermittently in the repertory at Lincoln's Inn Fields; however, it had never been performed at Drury Lane before the production Cibber describes. More troublesome is the song given in Appendix A which seems to point to a Drury Lane production of about this date but with Sir John still disguised as a parson.[3]

Still, Cibber's statement about the authorship of the scenes and date of revision is unequivocal, and he was in position to know. Alwin Thaler allows high merit to the revisions: ". . . the remarkable thing about the revision is that Sir John thus translated is, if anything, funnier than ever."[4] Here I cannot quite agree, and would like to think that some subordinate pen (Cibber's?) filled in what the aging Vanbrugh had outlined. There was no way of saving the pretense of probability that the earlier scenes had; the new ones are patently

[2] *An Apology for the Life of Colley Cibber*, ed. Robert W. Lowe (London 1889), II, 233.

[3] The most probable solution is that the song is misascribed to Harper. Harper presumably played Colonel Bully at Drury Lane (though the first cast detailed enough to list the part is September 15, 1726). The alternative is to assume that he played the part at Lincoln's Inn Fields during the two seasons, 1719–1721, that he was a member of that company. Drury Lane's advertisements in 1726 regularly stated, "Revised by the author." Lincoln's Inn Fields countered with its production on March 19, 1726, advertising "With new songs proper to the play, compos'd and sung by Leveridge and Legare." The song may have been one of these; in any case it seems likely that Drury Lane played the revised scenes, Lincoln's Inn Fields the original ones.

[4] *Representative English Comedies*, IV (New York, 1936), 422. Thaler (who supports the 1706 date) goes on to suggest that the idea came from a scene in *Squire Trelooby*, which was then being revived.

absurd. Sir John's description—totally unnecessary to the scene—of how a lady of quality spends the day is at best a tired reminiscence of Lord Foppington's account of his day in Act II of *The Relapse*. And morality is oddly served, for the new scenes are coarser and more indecent than the old. The lines are capable of being "gagged" further, and one interpolation has made its way into late acting texts; the parting of Sir John and the Justice concludes:

SIR JOHN. Mr. Justice, will you be so kind and obliging as to grant me one favor?

JUSTICE. Ay, what is it?

SIR JOHN. That your worship would be so very obliging as to let me have the honor of a chaste salute. Won't you?

JUSTICE. Good bye t'ye, madam.[5]

The following scenes are reprinted from the London edition of 1759. This text is not dependent upon the earlier Dublin edition and hence is of at least equal authority.[6]

[IV.i]   *Covent Garden.*
          Enter Lord Rake, Sir John, *&c., with swords drawn.*

LORD RAKE.
     Is the dog dead?
COLONEL BULLY.
     No, damn him, I heard him wheeze.
LORD RAKE.
     How the witch his wife howled!
COLONEL BULLY.
     Aye, she'll alarm the watch presently.
LORD RAKE.
     Appear, knight, then. Come, you have a good cause to fight
     for, there's a man murdered.
SIR JOHN.
     Is there? Then let his ghost be satisfied; for I'll sacrifice a

5 Here quoted from Mrs. Inchbald's *British Theatre* (London, 1808); most similar collections also have these lines.

6 These revised scenes were used for the London production of 1963. Kenneth Tynan, in his review for *The Observer* (July 28, 1963), commented: "The scenes in which this pathological woman-hater decides, for no good reason, to don his wife's new dress and let himself be arrested as 'Bonduca, the Queen of the Welchmen' are psychologically revealing as well as extremely funny."

constable to it presently, and burn his body upon his wooden chair.

Enter a Tailor *with a bundle under his arm.*

COLONEL BULLY.

How now, what have we got here, a thief?

TAILOR.

No, an't please you, I'm no thief.

LORD RAKE.

That we'll see presently. Here, let the general examine him.

SIR JOHN.

Aye, aye. Let me examine him, and I'll lay a hundred pound I find him guilty in spite of his teeth, for he looks—like a— sneaking rascal. Come sirrah, without equivocation or mental reservation, tell me of what opinion you are and what calling, for by them—I shall guess at your morals.

TAILOR.

An't please you, I'm a dissenting journeyman woman's tailor.

SIR JOHN.

Then sirrah, you love lying by your religion, and theft by your trade. And so that your punishment may be suitable to your crimes, I'll have you first gagged, and then hanged.

TAILOR.

Pray good worthy gentlemen, don't abuse me; indeed I'm an honest man and a good workman, though I say it that should not say it.

SIR JOHN.

No words, sirrah, but attend your fate.

LORD RAKE.

Let me see what's in that bundle.

TAILOR.

An't please you, it is my lady's short cloak and sack.

SIR JOHN.

What lady, you reptile you?

TAILOR.

My Lady Brute, an't please your honor.

SIR JOHN.

My Lady Brute! My wife! The robe of my wife; with reverence let me approach it. The dear angel is always taking care

of me in danger and has sent me this suit of armor to protect
me in this day of battle. On they go!

[ALL.]

O brave knight!

LORD RAKE.

Live Don Quixote the Second!

SIR JOHN.

Sancho, my squire, help me on with my armor.

TAILOR.

O dear gentlemen, I shall be quite undone if you take the
sack.

SIR JOHN.

Retire, sirrah. And since you carry off your skin, go home
and be happy.

TAILOR.

I think I'd e'en as good follow the gentleman's advice. For
if I dispute any longer, who knows but the whim may take
'em to case me. These courtiers are fuller of tricks than they
are of money; they'll sooner break a man's bones than pay
his bill.   *Exit.*

SIR JOHN.

So! How d'ye like my shapes now?

LORD RAKE.

To a miracle. He looks like a queen of the Amazons. But
to your arms, gentlemen! The enemy's upon their march;
here's the watch.

SIR JOHN.

Oons, if it were Alexander the Great at the head of his army,
I would drive him into a horse pond.

ALL.

Huzza! O brave knight!

Enter Watchmen.

SIR JOHN.

See, here he comes with all his Greeks about him. Follow
me, boys!

WATCHMAN.

Hey dey! Who have we got here? Stand!

SIR JOHN.

May hap not!

1 WATCHMAN.

What are you all doing here in the street at this time o'
night? And who are you, madam, that seem to be at the
head of this noble crew?

SIR JOHN.

Sirrah, I am Bonduca, Queen of the Welchmen; and with a
leek as long as my pedigree I will destroy your Roman
legion in an instant. Britons, strike home!

They fight off. Watchmen return with Sir John.

WATCHMAN.

So! We have got the queen, however. We'll make her pay
well for her ransom. Come, madam, will your majesty please
to walk before the constable?

SIR JOHN.

The constable's a rascal. And you are the son of a whore!

WATCHMAN.

A most noble reply, truly. If this be her royal style, I'll
warrant her maids of honor prattle prettily. But we'll teach
you some of our court dialect before we part with you,
princess. Away with her to the roundhouse!

SIR JOHN.

Hands off, you ruffians! My honor's dearer to me than my
life! I hope you won't be uncivil.

WATCHMAN.

Away with her. *Exeunt.*

[IV.iii] *A Street.*
Enter Constable *and* Watchmen *with* Sir John.

CONSTABLE.

Come, forsooth, come along if you please. I once in compassion thought to have seen you safe home this morning,
but you have been so rampant and abusive all night, I shall
see what the Justice of Peace will say to you.

SIR JOHN.

And you shall see what I'll say to the Justice of Peace.

Watchman *knocks at the door.*

Enter Servant.

CONSTABLE.

Is Mr. Justice at home?

SERVANT.

Yes.

CONSTABLE.

Pray acquaint his worship we have got an unruly woman here and desire to know what he'll please to have done with her.

SERVANT.

I'll acquaint my master. *Exit.*

SIR JOHN.

Hark you, Constable, what cuckoldly Justice is this?

CONSTABLE.

One that knows how to deal with such romps as you are, I'll warrant you.

Enter Justice.

JUSTICE.

Well, Mr. Constable, what is the matter there?

CONSTABLE.

An't please your worship, this here comical sort of a gentlewoman has committed great outrages tonight. She has been frolicking with my Lord Rake and his gang; they attacked the watch and I hear there has been a man killed; I believe 'tis they have done it.

SIR JOHN.

Sir, there may have been murder for aught I know. And 'tis a great mercy there has not been a rape too; that fellow would have ravished me.

2 WATCHMAN.

Ravish! Ravish! O lud, O lud, O lud. Ravish her! Why, please your worship, I heard Mr. Constable say he believed she was little better than a maphrodrite.

JUSTICE.

Why truly, she does seem a little masculine about the mouth.

2 WATCHMAN.

Yes, and about the hands too, an't please your worship. I did but offer in mere civility to help her up the steps into our apartment, and with her gripen fist—aye, just so, sir—

Sir John *knocks him down.*

SIR JOHN.

I felled him to the ground like an ox.

JUSTICE.

Out upon this boisterous woman! Out upon her!

SIR JOHN.

Mr. Justice, he would have been uncivil. It was in defense of my honor, and I demand satisfaction.

2 WATCHMAN.

I hope your worship will satisfy her honor in Bridewell. That fist of hers will make an admirable hemp-beater.

SIR JOHN.

Sir, I hope you will protect me against that libidinous rascal; I am a woman of quality and virtue, too, for all I am in an undress this morning.

JUSTICE.

Why, she has really the air of a sort of a woman a little something out of the common.—Madam, if you expect I should be favorable to you, I desire I may know who you are.

SIR JOHN.

Sir, I am anybody, at your service.

JUSTICE.

Lady, I desire to know your name.

SIR JOHN.

Sir, my name's Mary.

JUSTICE.

Aye, but your surname, madam?

SIR JOHN.

Sir, my surname's the same with my husband's.

JUSTICE.

A strange woman, this! Who is your husband, pray?

SIR JOHN.

Sir John.

JUSTICE.

Sir John who?

SIR JOHN.

Sir John Brute.

JUSTICE.

Is it possible, madam, you can be my Lady Brute?

SIR JOHN.

That happy woman, sir, am I; only a little in my merriment tonight.

JUSTICE.

I am concerned for Sir John.

SIR JOHN.

Truly, so am I.

JUSTICE.

I have heard he's an honest gentleman—

SIR JOHN.

As ever drank.

JUSTICE.

Good lack! Indeed, lady, I'm sorry he has such a wife.

SIR JOHN.

I am sorry he has any wife at all.

JUSTICE.

And so perhaps may he. I doubt you have not given him a very good taste of matrimony.

SIR JOHN.

Taste, sir! Sir, I have scorned to stint him to a taste; I have given him a full meal of it.

JUSTICE.

Indeed, I believe so. But pray, fair lady, may he have given you any occasion for this extraordinary conduct? Does he not use you well?

SIR JOHN.

A little upon the rough, sometimes.

JUSTICE.

Aye, any man may be out of humor now and then.

SIR JOHN.

Sir, I love peace and quiet, and when a woman don't find that at home she's apt sometimes to comfort herself with a few innocent diversions abroad.

JUSTICE.

I doubt he uses you but too well. Pray how does he as to that weighty thing, money? Does he allow you what is proper of that?

SIR JOHN.

Sir, I have generally enough to pay the reckoning, if this son of a whore of a drawer would but bring his bill.

JUSTICE.

A strange woman this. Does he spend a reasonable portion of his time at home, to the comfort of his wife and children?

SIR JOHN.

He never gave his wife cause to repine at his being abroad in his life.

JUSTICE.

Pray madam, how may he be in the grand matrimonial point: is he true to your bed?

SIR JOHN.

Chaste! Ooons, this fellow asks so many impertinent questions, egad, I believe it is the Justice's wife in the Justice's clothes.

JUSTICE.

'Tis a great pity he should have been thus disposed of. Pray madam (and then I've done), what may be your ladyship's common method of life, if I may presume so far?

SIR JOHN.

Why sir, much like that of a woman of quality.

JUSTICE.

Pray how may you generally pass your time, madam? Your morning, for example?

SIR JOHN.

Sir, like a woman of quality. I wake about two o'clock in the afternoon, I stretch and make a sign for my chocolate. When I have drank three cups, I slide down again upon my back with my arms over my head, while my two maids put on my stockings. Then hanging upon their shoulders I am trailed to my great chair, where I sit, and yawn, for my breakfast. If it don't come presently, I lie down upon my couch to say my prayers, while my maid reads me the playbills.

JUSTICE.

Very well, madam.

SIR JOHN.

When the tea is brought in, I drink twelve regular dishes, with eight slices of bread and butter. And half an hour after, I send to the cook to know if the dinner is almost ready.

JUSTICE.

So, madam.

SIR JOHN.

By that time my head is half dressed, I hear my husband swearing himself into a state of perdition that the meat's all cold upon the table; to amend which, I come down in an hour more and have it sent back to the kitchen to be dressed all over again.

JUSTICE.

Poor man!

SIR JOHN.

When I have dined, and my idle servants are presumptuously set down at their ease to do so too, I call for my coach, go visit fifty dear friends, of whom I hope I shall never find one at home while I shall live.

JUSTICE.

So, there's the morning and afternoon pretty well disposed of. Pray madam, how do you pass your evenings?

SIR JOHN.

Like a woman of spirit, sir, a great spirit. Give me a box and dice—seven's the main. Oons, sir, I set you a hundred pound! Why, do you think women are married nowadays to sit at home and mend napkins? Sir, we have nobler ways of passing time.

JUSTICE.

Mercy upon us, Mr. Constable, what will this age come to?

CONSTABLE.

What will it come to, indeed, if such women as these are not set in the stocks?

SIR JOHN.

Sir, I have a little urgent business calls upon me, and therefore I desire the favor of you to bring matters to a conclusion.

JUSTICE.

Madam, if I were sure that business were not to commit more disorders, I would release you.

SIR JOHN.

None, by my virtue.

JUSTICE.

Then, Mr. Constable, you may discharge her.

SIR JOHN.

Sir, your very humble servant. If you please to accept of a bottle—

JUSTICE.

I thank you kindly madam, but I never drink in a morning. Goodbye t'ye, madam, goodbye t'ye.

SIR JOHN.

Goodbye t'ye, good sir.   *Exit* Justice.

So, now, Mr. Constable, shall you and I go pick up a whore together?

CONSTABLE.

No, thank you, madam; my wife's enough to satisfy any reasonable man.

SIR JOHN (*aside*).

He, he, he, he, he! The fool is married, then. Well, you won't go?

CONSTABLE.

Not I, truly.

SIR JOHN.

Then I'll go by myself; and you and your wife may be damned. *Exit* Sir John.

CONSTABLE (*gazing after her*).

Why, God a-mercy, my lady. *Exeunt.*

Appendix C

Chronology

Approximate dates are indicated by *. Dates for plays are those on which they were first made public, either on stage or in print.

Political and Literary Events	Life and Major Works of Vanbrugh

Political and Literary Events

1631
Death of Donne.
John Dryden born.

1633
Samuel Pepys born.

1635
Sir George Etherege born.*

1640
Aphra Behn born.*

1641
William Wycherley born.*

1642
First Civil War began (ended 1646).
Theaters closed by Parliament.
Thomas Shadwell born.*

1648
Second Civil War.
Nathaniel Lee born.*

1649
Execution of Charles I.

1650
Jeremy Collier born.

1651
Hobbes' *Leviathan* published.

1652
First Dutch War began (ended 1654).
Thomas Otway born.

1656
D'Avenant's *THE SIEGE OF RHODES* performed at Rutland House.

1657
John Dennis born.

1658
Death of Oliver Cromwell.
D'Avenant's *THE CRUELTY OF THE SPANIARDS IN PERU* performed at the Cockpit.

1660
Restoration of Charles II.
Theatrical patents granted to Thomas Killigrew and Sir William D'Avenant, authorizing them to form, respectively, the King's and the Duke of York's Companies.
Pepys began his diary.

1661
Cowley's *THE CUTTER OF COLEMAN STREET.*
D'Avenant's *THE SIEGE OF RHODES* (expanded to two parts).

1662
Charter granted to the Royal Society.

1663
Dryden's *THE WILD GALLANT.*
Tuke's *THE ADVENTURES OF FIVE HOURS.*

1664
Dryden's *THE RIVAL LADIES.* Born in London, January.
Dryden and Howard's *THE INDIAN QUEEN.*
Etherege's *THE COMICAL REVENGE.*

1665
Second Dutch War began (ended 1667).
Great Plague.

Dryden's *THE INDIAN EM-
PEROR.*
Orrery's *MUSTAPHA.*

1666
Fire of London.   Family moves to Chester.*
Death of James Shirley.

1667
Jonathan Swift born.
Milton's *Paradise Lost* published.
Sprat's *The History of the Royal
Society* published.
Dryden's *SECRET LOVE.*

1668
Death of D'Avenant.
Dryden made Poet Laureate.
Dryden's *An Essay of Dramatic
Poesy* published.
Shadwell's *THE SULLEN LOVERS.*

1669
Pepys terminated his diary.
Susannah Centlivre born.

1670
William Congreve born.
Dryden's *THE CONQUEST OF
GRANADA,* Part I.

1671
Dorset Garden Theatre (Duke's
Company) opened.
Colley Cibber born.
Milton's *Paradise Regained* and *Sam-
son Agonistes* published.
Dryden's *THE CONQUEST OF
GRANADA,* Part II.
THE REHEARSAL, by the Duke
of Buckingham and others.
Wycherley's *LOVE IN A WOOD.*

1672
Third Dutch War began (ended
1674).
Joseph Addison born.
Richard Steele born.
Dryden's *MARRIAGE A LA MODE.*

1674
New Drury Lane Theatre (King's
Company) opened.
Death of Milton.
Nicholas Rowe born.
Thomas Rymer's *Reflections on Aris-
totle's Treatise of Poesy* (translation
of Rapin) published.

1675
Dryden's *AURENG-ZEBE.*
Wycherley's *THE COUNTRY
WIFE.**

1676
Etherege's *THE MAN OF MODE.*
Otway's *DON CARLOS.*
Shadwell's *THE VIRTUOSO.*
Wycherley's *THE PLAIN DEALER.*

1677
Aphra Behn's *THE ROVER.*
Dryden's *ALL FOR LOVE.*
Lee's *THE RIVAL QUEENS.*
Rymer's *Tragedies of the Last Age
Considered* published.

1678
Popish Plot.
George Farquhar born.
Bunyan's *Pilgrim's Progress* (Part I)
published.

1679
Exclusion Bill introduced.
Death of Thomas Hobbes.
Death of Roger Boyle, Earl of
Orrery.
Charles Johnson born.

1680
Death of Samuel Butler.
Death of John Wilmot, Earl of
Rochester.
Dryden's *THE SPANISH FRIAR.*
Lee's *LUCIUS JUNIUS BRUTUS.*
Otway's *THE ORPHAN.*

1681

Charles II dissolved Parliament at Oxford.

Dryden's *Absalom and Achitophel* published.

Tate's adaptation of *KING LEAR.*

1682

The King's and the Duke of York's Companies merged into the United Company.

Dryden's *The Medal, MacFlecknoe,* and *Religio Laici* published.

Otway's *VENICE PRESERVED.*

1683

Rye House Plot.

Death of Thomas Killigrew.

Crowne's *CITY POLITIQUES.*

1685

Death of Charles II; accession of James II.

Revocation of the Edict of Nantes.

The Duke of Monmouth's Rebellion.

Death of Otway.

John Gay born.

Crowne's *SIR COURTLY NICE.*

Dryden's *ALBION AND ALBANIUS.*

1686

Commissioned Ensign in Lord Huntington's regiment.

1687

Death of the Duke of Buckingham.

Dryden's *The Hind and the Panther* published.

Newton's *Principia* published.

1688

The Revolution.

Arrested and imprisoned at Calais.

Alexander Pope born.

Shadwell's *THE SQUIRE OF ALSATIA.*

1689

The War of the League of Augsburg
began (ended 1697).
Toleration Act.
Death of Aphra Behn.
Shadwell made Poet Laureate.
Dryden's *DON SEBASTIAN*.
Shadwell's *BURY FAIR*.

1690

Battle of the Boyne.
Locke's *Two Treatises of Government*
and *An Essay Concerning Human
Understanding* published.

1691

Death of Etherege.   Transferred to Vincennes.
Langbaine's *An Account of the
English Dramatic Poets* published.

1692

Death of Lee.   Transferred to Bastille, January;
Death of Shadwell.   released and returned to England,
Tate made Poet Laureate.   November.

1693

George Lillo born.
Rymer's *A Short View of Tragedy*
published.
Congreve's *THE OLD BACHELOR*.

1694

Death of Queen Mary.
Southerne's *THE FATAL MAR-
RIAGE*.

1695

Group of actors led by Thomas
Betterton left Drury Lane and estab-
lished a new company at Lincoln's
Inn Fields.
Congreve's *LOVE FOR LOVE*.
Southerne's *OROONOKO*.

1696

Cibber's *LOVE'S LAST SHIFT*.   Appointed Captain in Lord Berke-
ley's regiment.
THE RELAPSE (Drury Lane,
November 21).
AESOP (Drury Lane, December).

1697

Treaty of Ryswick ended the War of the League of Augsburg.
Charles Macklin born.
Congreve's *THE MOURNING BRIDE*.

AESOP, Part II (Drury Lane, April).
THE PROVOKED WIFE (Lincoln's Inn Fields, April).

1698

Collier controversy started with the publication of *A Short View of the Immorality and Profaneness of the English Stage*.

A Short Vindication of The Relapse and the Provok'd Wife from Immorality and Prophaneness published.
THE COUNTRY HOUSE (Drury Lane, January).

1699

Farquhar's *THE CONSTANT COUPLE*.

Appointed architect for Castle Howard.

1700

Death of Dryden.
Blackmore's *Satire against Wit* published.
Congreve's *THE WAY OF THE WORLD*.

THE PILGRIM, altered from Fletcher, with masque by Dryden (Drury Lane, April).

1701

Act of Settlement.
War of the Spanish Succession began (ended 1713).
Death of James II.
Rowe's *TAMERLANE*.
Steele's *THE FUNERAL*.

1702

Death of William III; accession of Anne.
The Daily Courant began publication.
Cibber's *SHE WOULD AND SHE WOULD NOT*.

Appointed Comptroller to the Board of Works.
THE FALSE FRIEND (Drury Lane, February).

1703

Death of Samuel Pepys.
Rowe's *THE FAIR PENITENT*.

Appointed Carlisle Herald.
Begins construction of Haymarket Theatre.

1704

Capture of Gibraltar; Battle of Blenheim.
Defoe's *The Review* began publication (1704–1713).

Appointed Clarenceux King-at-Arms.
SQUIRE TRELOOBY, with Congreve and Walsh (Lincoln's

Swift's *A Tale of a Tub and The Battle of the Books* published.
Cibber's *THE CARELESS HUSBAND*.

Inn Fields, April 30).

1705
Haymarket Theatre opened.
Steele's *THE TENDER HUSBAND*.

Appointed architect for Blenheim Palace.
In management of Haymarket Theatre, with Congreve.
THE CONFEDERACY (Haymarket, November 30).
THE MISTAKE (Haymarket, December 27).

1706
Battle of Ramillies.
Farquhar's *THE RECRUITING OFFICER*.

Visits Hanover as herald.
Begins withdrawal from management of Haymarket.

1707
Union of Scotland and England.
Death of Farquhar.
Henry Fielding born.
Farquhar's *THE BEAUX' STRATAGEM*.

Appointed to restore Kimbolton Castle.
THE CUCKOLD IN CONCEIT (Haymarket, March 22), unpublished.

1708
Downes' *Roscius Anglicanus* published.

1709
Samuel Johnson born.
Rowe's edition of Shakespeare published.
The Tatler began publication (1709–1711).
Centlivre's *THE BUSY BODY*.

1710

Designed King's Weston.*

1711
Shaftesbury's *Characteristics* published.
The Spectator began publication (1711–1712).
Pope's *An Essay on Criticism* published.

1713

Treaty of Utrecht ended the War of the Spanish Succession.
Addison's *CATO*.

Dismissed as Comptroller to the Board of Works (reappointed 1715).

1714

Death of Anne; accession of George I.
Steele became Governor of Drury Lane.
John Rich assumed management of Lincoln's Inn Fields.
Centlivre's *THE WONDER: A WOMAN KEEPS A SECRET*.
Rowe's *JANE SHORE*.

Knighted by George I.

1715

Jacobite Rebellion.
Death of Tate.
Rowe made Poet Laureate.
Death of Wycherley.

Appointed architect for Greenwich Hospital.

1716

Addison's *THE DRUMMER*.

Begins designs for Eastbury.*

1717

David Garrick born.
Cibber's *THE NON-JUROR*. Gay, Pope, and Arbuthnot's *THREE HOURS AFTER MARRIAGE*.

1718

Death of Rowe.
Centlivre's *A BOLD STROKE FOR A WIFE*.

Designed Floors Castle.

1719

Death of Addison.
Defoe's *Robinson Crusoe* published.
Young's *BUSIRIS, KING OF EGYPT*.

Married Henrietta Maria Yarborough.
Plays, two volumes, published.

1720

South Sea Bubble.
Samuel Foote born.
Steele suspended from the Governorship of Drury Lane (restored 1721).

A son, Charles Vanbrugh, born May 12.
Appointed architect for Seaton Delaval.

Appendix C

Little Theatre in the Haymarket
opened.
Steele's *The Theatre* (periodical)
published.
Hughes' *THE SIEGE OF DAMAS-
CUS*.

1721
Walpole became first Minister.   Appointed to restore Audley End.

1722
Steele's *THE CONSCIOUS
LOVERS*.

1723
Death of Susannah Centlivre.
Death of D'Urfey

1725
Pope's edition of Shakespeare published.

1726
Death of Jeremy Collier.   Died March 26.
Law's *Unlawfulness of Stage Enter-
tainments* published.
Swift's *Gulliver's Travels* published.

1727
Death of George I; accession of
George II.
Death of Sir Isaac Newton.
Arthur Murphy born.

1728
Pope's *The Dunciad* (first version)   *THE PROVOKED HUSBAND*,
published. Gay's *THE BEGGAR'S*   Cibber's completion of the fragmen-
OPERA.   tary *A JOURNEY TO LONDON*
(Drury Lane, January 10).

1729
Goodman's Fields Theatre opened.
Death of Congreve.
Death of Steele.
Edmund Burke born.

1730
Cibber made Poet Laureate.
Oliver Goldsmith born.
Thomson's *The Seasons* published.

Fielding's *THE AUTHOR'S FARCE.*

Fielding's *TOM THUMB* (revised as *THE TRAGEDY OF TRAGEDIES,* 1731).

1731

Death of Defoe.

Fielding's *THE GRUB-STREET OPERA.*

Lillo's *THE LONDON MERCHANT.*

1732

Covent Garden Theatre opened.

Death of Gay.

George Colman the elder born.

Fielding's *THE COVENT GARDEN TRAGEDY.*

Fielding's *THE MODERN HUSBAND.*

Charles Johnson's *CAELIA.*

1733

Pope's *An Essay on Man* (Epistles I–III) published (Epistle IV, 1734).

1734

Death of Dennis.

The Prompter began publication (1734–1736).

Theobald's edition of Shakespeare published.

Fielding's *DON QUIXOTE IN ENGLAND.*

1736

Fielding led the "Great Mogul's Company of Comedians" at the Little Theatre in the Haymarket (1736–1737).

Fielding's *PASQUIN.*

Lillo's *FATAL CURIOSITY.*

1737

The Stage Licensing Act.

Dodsley's *THE KING AND THE MILLER OF MANSFIELD.*

Fielding's *THE HISTORICAL REGISTER FOR* 1736.